THE
DIRT ROAD

ISBN:979-8-9996242-1-5
Printed in the United States of America.

THE DIRT ROAD

A Story of Family, Forgiveness, and Finding Your Way Home

by Robert Hendry

TABLE OF CONTENTS

Author's Note:

This book is a true account of my life, drawn from memory, reflection, and the emotional imprint of growing up in a world shaped by addiction, mental illness, and love in its most complicated forms.

I didn't write *The Dirt Road* to cast blame or dwell in pain—I wrote it to honor the truth, and to offer hope to anyone who has ever felt alone, unseen, or unsure if their past could ever lead to a future worth fighting for.

If you've lived through hard things, I hope you find something here that helps you feel less alone. And if you haven't, I hope this book helps you understand those who have.

We all have our own roads to navigate. This is mine.

—Robert Hendry

Prologue:

GOOD TIMES, BAD TIMES

I grew up on a dirt road in rural South Georgia, just outside of Savannah.

To some, that might sound idyllic—fireflies at dusk, sweet tea on the porch, bare feet in the summer dust. But for me, that road was never just a road. It was a boundary line between chaos and calm. Between the life I was born into and the one I dreamed of finding.

Out there, beyond the noise of town and the watchful eyes of family neighbors, things happened that most people didn't see. Doors slammed. Words cut. Bottles clinked. There were nights I lay awake in fear, days I walked on eggshells, moments I wondered if I'd ever feel safe in my own skin.

But somehow, I kept going.

The dirt road taught me a lot. How to keep secrets. How to scan a room the moment I walked in. How to hold back tears, even when I felt like screaming. But it also taught me how to survive. How to hold on to hope when everything around me felt like it was falling apart.

This book isn't just a story about a boy from the South. It's a story about what happens when the people who are supposed to protect you can't—or won't. It's about navigating grief, addiction, violence, and betrayal—and still believing that life can offer something more. Something better.

The Dirt Road is about how I got here—scarred but standing. It's about the moments that shaped me, the people who helped me, and the strength I didn't know I had until life demanded it from me.

If you're walking your own road, dirt or paved, I hope these pages remind you that you're not alone. That your story matters. And that even the roughest roads can lead to something better.

Because sometimes, the road you start on isn't the one you stay on.

And sometimes, the dirt road is where the real journey begins.

Chapter 1:

AMERICAN PIE

The first time I knew something was wrong, I was six years old, standing outside my parents' bedroom door, pressing my ear against a wall of smoke and secrets.

I'd knocked because I was lonely. I missed them. I thought maybe they'd forgotten I was out there.

Instead, I got a gust of air that stung my eyes and made my throat close up.

"Go back to the living room," my father barked. And the door slammed shut.

That moment would come to define so much more than I realized. But before all that—before the loneliness and confusion—there was music.

One of my earliest memories is of sitting in our tiny living room wearing headphones twice the size of my head, singing along to The Monkees

The vinyl crackled faintly under the needle before the bassline kicked in, vibrating through the thick wood floor with a thin layer of brown shag carpet, beneath my bare feet. The headphones were heavy, the faux leather pads warm against my ears, smelling faintly of plastic and dust.

"Hey, hey, we're the Monkees, and people say we monkey around. But we're too busy singing, to put anybody down."

My parents' speakers flanking the stereo were taller than I was. The spiral cord attached to the headphones seemed to stretch for miles. We tend to think of most things as gigantic when we're under the age of ten, and it's not until later in life that we realize these items weren't really large at all. Still, electronics back then *were* huge. Each speaker was encased in deep brown wood, darkened by layers of varnish, etched with scratches from years of use.

Stacked between them was a massive wooden shelving unit that housed what seemed like an endless collection of vinyl records. Just name a southern, classic, or hard rock band from the '60s or '70s, and you'd find their albums there. I remember sitting on a stool in nothing but my underwear, singing along, completely lost in the moment. I also remember the prideful embarrassment I felt when I noticed my mother watching from the kitchen—smiling and chuckling, quietly amused. That was a very happy time.

3

Sometimes I sit down and look at old photographs from that period and am amazed at how happy we looked. Life seemed so simple. Although I was an only child, I had a vivid imagination and spent countless hours playing outside in the backyard. Some days I was an elite soldier on a mission to save hostages in a war-torn foreign land. Other days, I was Indiana Jones, making my way through ancient civilizations in search of a treasured lost relic. Even rainy days couldn't stop me. I'd grab a pocket handkerchief from my dad's dresser drawer, fold it, tie it behind my head, and become an Apache warrior ready to attack.

In those early years, my imagination was my fortress. But soon, I'd learn some battles couldn't be won by pretending.

On Saturday mornings, I loved watching cartoons. I'd lie there on the couch, entrenched in the colorful world of happy chaos. My mom used to sing to the radio while she cooked breakfast—sometimes Fleetwood Mac, sometimes Whitney Houston, depending on her mood.

We didn't have much, but we had rhythm. Traditions. Predictability. My baseball glove was always on the dresser. My dad's boots were always by the door. And most nights, we ate dinner together.

But then, things got... quieter. At first, I didn't notice. I only realized it had been a while since I'd heard Mom sing. Or that Dad had started falling asleep on the couch with the TV blaring, still in his work clothes. Dinner got later. Sometimes it didn't happen at all.

I didn't know what to call it back then, but the air in our house started to feel thicker. Like, there was something unspoken sitting at the dinner table with us. I'd try to keep things normal—talk about Ninja Turtles, or how many baseball cards I'd collected—but more often than not, my words felt like pebbles dropped into a well. No splash. No echo. Just quiet.

One Christmas in the early 1980's I woke up to the sound of a whimper coming from the living room. I quickly jumped out of bed, bewildered by what it could be. I rushed down the hallway to discover a beautiful Collie puppy, just like Lassie inside of a compressed wood treasure chest toybox. I instantly named him Chip after the TV show Chips. It was one of my favorites. His fur was soft and wild, like worn-out shag carpet. His bark was still a puppy yelp—high and uncoordinated. We'd tumble in the grass until we were both out of breath. To this day, I can still remember lying underneath the coffee table playing with He-man action figures with Chip by my side. Chip was my first best friend and he was the best dog a boy could ask for.

At four years old, I started playing baseball. I instantly fell in love with the game and the excitement of playing with other kids. Back home, I had a sandbox, a bicycle, horseshoes, cap-guns—and parents and grandparents who loved me. So, in my mind, I was rich.

At five years old, I saw snow for the first and only time in person, until later in my adult years. I can remember bundling up in a jacket, gloves, a wool hat

6

and extra socks before I stepped outside to watch the mystical flakes falling down. It was so quiet I could hear the flakes landing, like the tiniest whispers. My cheeks tingled as the cold kissed them. It was cold enough that the snow was able to stick to the ground for one night. I even built a small snowman with my mother.

Unfortunately, those distant memories that stand out are few and far between. That handful of years before things began to fall apart and crumble were certainly too short.

Not long after that summer, the mood began to shift.

I was in my room playing with G.I. Joes when I heard a knock at the door. My grandfather's voice called out joyfully. "Robbie!"

My dad echoed him. "Hey, Robbie, come outside. Your grandfather wants to see you."

Outside, my grandfather, George "Thurmond" Hendry, was beaming. He had something to show me. We lived off Highway 280 in a very small community in South Georgia called Ellabell, and right beside our property was a tiny waste center we called "the dump." There were no recycling centers back then—just places to toss what you no longer needed. Once a week or so the County would process everything that had built up and then the process would start all over again. But to my grandfather, that dump was a gold-mine. He had a knack for finding value in other people's trash. And this time, he'd struck gold.

He found a discarded blue 4x4 Bigfoot Power Wheel. It didn't work. But that didn't matter. He brought it home, cleaned it up, and with a little ingenuity—and a car battery—he got it running again. And let me tell you, that car battery gave it way more juice than the original ever could.

Thurmond was a retired Air Force officer. He had spent many years in the military serving as a training instructor and served all over the world. He had been stationed in Shreveport Louisiana when my father was born, served in Germany when my father was a child, and even served at McCoy Air Force Base, which Orlando's airport is now named after and sits on part of the land where McCoy AFB once stood. He had a knack for turning metal and parts into magic.

The first time I hit the gas, it jerked forward so fast I thought I might fall out—my stomach did a flip and I squealed in delight as the wind slapped my cheeks.

I must have ridden that thing for hours and days on end in the field between our house and my grandparents'. Pure joy. But that season of fun and freedom soon gave way to something darker.

I didn't understand what drugs were at such an early age. I knew my parents had a bad habit of smoking cigarettes, and my father drank beer every day. But the concept of other substances that altered your mind or behavior was completely foreign to me.

That, however, began to change — slowly at first, then all at once.

Even though I was young and naïve, I had emotions. Childhood emotions are often raw and undeveloped, but they're real just the same. I understood excitement, joy, pain, and hurt in my own way.

Each day, my parents would disappear into their bedroom for about thirty minutes, stuffing a blanket under the door before closing it. The edges of the blanket stuck out like tongues of smoke, stained and sagging from repeated use. I'd be left sitting in the living room alone, wondering why. And wondering what I'd done wrong. "Why are they shutting me out?" I would think. "Do they not love me?"

The silence in the room afterward wasn't peaceful—it was vacant, echoey, like the walls had swallowed up my parents and left ghosts in their place.

One day, I built up the courage to knock on the door and tell them I was sad they'd left me out.

When the door opened, a wall of smoke hit me like a punch to the stomach. The smell was sharp, sour — it took my breath away.

They'd been sneaking off to smoke marijuana. I didn't understand that at the time, but I knew something wasn't right.

Their personalities changed. They'd come out of that room acting light and careless — almost like teenagers. But even as a child, I could feel something was off. Somehow, I felt more grounded than they were. More responsible.

I didn't have the words for it back then. But deep down, I knew: This wasn't how it was supposed to be. I knew it was wrong and it made me angry. I developed a disdain for drugs and at that early age made a vow to myself that I would never touch a drug or be involved with something that influenced me, in a way that pushed the people I loved away. And that feeling has stuck with me through all these years.

Later that year, my grandmother Mary was diagnosed with breast cancer. Back then, cancer felt like a death sentence. I remember the adults having serious conversations about it. My dad and his two brothers would talk quietly with my grandparents. It all seemed so complex.

She began chemotherapy, and I watched it take its toll. Still, she was strong. Always strong. She kept smiling, kept cooking, kept living.

Then came a moment I'll never forget.

She and my grandfather came home from a doctor's visit carrying bags of Krystal burgers—one of my favorites. I waited eagerly in their dining room, sitting at the long wooden table where we would often eat as a family, including my father's two younger brothers. Then my grandmother looked at me and said, "Robbie, I need to show you something."

She lifted her wig and revealed her bald head, laughing as she said, "I'm fully bald now, just like an old man!"

My grandmother was unique—unlike any woman I knew. She was tall and tough, but also graceful. She had raised three boys and knew how to hold her ground, but she also knew how to nurture and show her love in quiet, intentional ways.

I loved going to Savannah with her because she always had a nicer car than anyone else I rode with, and she made sure to treat me like I was special. Early on, she started a tradition of taking me shopping at the PX on base at Fort Stewart. Every year, no matter the cost, she bought me a brand-new pair of shoes for school. I always picked out the latest Jordans—even though the rest of my clothes weren't name brand, those shoes made me feel like I was special.

It was her way of lightening the moment. But I wasn't ready. I burst into tears—overwhelmed by the sudden, real reminder that the people I loved weren't immortal. That they could hurt. That they could die.

My mom said it was inappropriate—that my grandmother had crossed a line exposing me to something so raw. I understand her reaction now. Mothers are protective. But part of me still wonders if that moment was the tipping point—the straw that broke the camel's back in their already fragile relationship.

Strangely, I have only a handful of those memories—good or bad—from before age ten. Sometimes I wonder if most people remember more from their childhood, or if it's common to only recall scattered fragments. My dad can remember living in Germany as a young boy while my grandfather was stationed there. He tells those stories quite vividly. I listen and wonder why mine feel so distant. So dim.

What I do remember clearly is the beginning of the rift between my mother and my grandmother—and her mother, my great-grandmother Granny Byrnside. Once it started, it never stopped. It didn't matter if we were headed to the grocery store, post office, or the beach. Long car rides turned into therapy sessions, with my mother venting to me, unloading frustrations

15

that I wasn't equipped to process, and asking me what she should do. I was just a kid—scared, confused, unsure how to comfort her.

But I tried. I always tried.

Eventually, I became good at listening. At reasoning. At absorbing emotions that weren't mine. Over time, those conversations started to color how I saw my grandmother, too. It was complicated— because at that time, I had a very close relationship with her. I was the only grandchild on my father's side of the family, which meant all the attention, all the love. Being with her felt like wrapping up in a warm blanket on a rainy day. But I also felt deep down that my mother's feelings and concerns, while they might be overblown, were probably valid in some sort of way.

Looking back, I imagine there was more to the story. My father was the oldest, and he'd married a woman from a very different world. His parents were middle class—composed, structured, proud. My mom came from a dirt-poor, salt-of-the-earth family with seven kids, raised in a homestead passed down since 1845.

Maybe my grandmother and great-grandmother looked down on her. Maybe my mother had always felt like an outsider and projected that onto herself. Maybe both things were true.

Time is strange. Like those childhood objects that once felt so massive, it moves differently depending on your age. As a kid, it drips like molasses. But looking back, those last years living next to my father's parents blur together in a flash—like the final grains of sand racing through an hourglass.

And just like that... it was over.

THE DIRT ROAD

Chapter 2:

TELL ME 'BOUT THE GOOD 'OL DAYS

We didn't pack to start a new adventure—we packed to escape reality.

I don't recall my parents first telling me that we were going to move. But I do remember that one of the driving factors was the fact that my uncle Royce, my father's middle brother, had gotten married and announced they were having twins.

As the pregnancy progressed, they learned that the twins would be two little girls. Amanda and VaRanda were going to be their names. I can still see my grandmother's eyes lighting up with joy at the news that she would have not one, but two granddaughters. Her life's work of raising three boys was taking shape. They were starting families of their own. She was happy and proud.

What I also noticed was the gleam in my mother's eyes beginning to fade, replaced by an air of envy, resentment, and jealousy. In my mind, I believed she justified developing those feelings on my behalf. To protect me. It was as if I would no longer be the center of attention, no longer receive the same love and nourishment from my grandmother.

At the baby shower my mother put on a smiling face. But I knew she wasn't happy that evening. I remember overhearing her whisper sharply to my dad that night after the visit, "It's all about the twins now." It didn't seem like a joke.

She began to complain at home, more and more, about how my grandmother Mary was treating her. It got to the point that my dad finally gave in to the idea of moving. To escape. To get away.

In retrospect, I'm not sure if those were her true feelings or just my interpretation. I never felt any less love from my grandmother. Her pride in the twins never bothered me; it seemed like a natural response for any grandparent.

What made things worse was that my uncle had purchased a new trailer and placed it right next to ours in the large, open grassy area across from my grandparents' house. Just as they had shared their property with my father, they did the same for Royce. That added a whole new level of tension. Now, every time she looked out the window, there was Royce's new trailer—shiny, modern, planted like a flag in territory she once thought was hers.

Once my father was on board with the idea, my mom started talking to her parents about the situation. They didn't have shiny things, but they had lots of land. So, my grandfather offered my parents an acre behind their house situated on the long dirt road that ran between my grandmother Helen's property and her sister Ruby's property. The land had been passed down to them from their father many years prior.

The acre of land also sat on the far side of the small field next to my grandparent's house that we had worked each spring and summer prior.

I was ten years old when we moved—just before the summer of 1991. Amanda and VaRanda had just been born one week after my birthday, but it was the baby shower that had set things in motion.

I remember moving day vividly. I had a wooden playhouse with a tin roof that my father had built from scrap wood he purchased at a steep discount from his job. He was a kiln operator at the local Georgia Pacific sawmill. They always had deals on lumber that didn't make the final cut—no pun intended. My father, like his father, had a knack for finding a good deal. The boards were in random sized pieces, mostly ranging four to six feet long. This added a lot of character to the structure. It looked well-built when finished, but the variation in sizes added an aged, rustic look to it.

The playhouse was intended to be a treehouse, though it sat only about two feet off the ground. It had two windows, a small loft area, and tons of storage space for things like my cap guns, baseball bats, random parts and pieces I had commandeered from my grandfather's junk pile that resembled some type of object I needed for my adventures, and handmade items like homemade handcuffs I had fashioned out of tiny shaved-down branches.

23

Moving it wasn't easy, but my father and grandfather managed. They cut the legs off at the bottom since it had been secured with concrete in the ground, used a jack to raise it, and slid a flatbed trailer beneath.

Watching the trailer rolling across the field felt surreal. Our home, having been something permanent in my mind, was being whisked away with effort and ease. I can still see my grandfather backing in to connect the trailer, carefully maneuvering it out of the narrow driveway as I stood watching from twenty-five feet away. And just like that, the spot at the far end of my grandparent's property where our home used to sit was empty. The only thing that remained was a rectangular patch of dirt where no grass had grown due to not receiving sunlight.

Later that day, over at my mother's parents' house, our new property had already been surveyed and prepped. A shallow well and septic tank had been installed, and the homesite was ready. It sat just behind my grandparents' house, encroaching on part of the old field where my grandfather, Ralph "Cooter" Davis, planted corn, squash, peas, butterbeans, and watermelon. That plot was about three or four acres— his smaller field. His larger field, directly across the street from his house, was twenty acres of crops surrounded by another five acres of woods. It was a secluded, country oasis.

I had mixed emotions about the move. I was incredibly close to my grandmother and I knew the move meant that I would no longer see her every day as I had for the last ten years. I had grown so accustomed to visiting my grandmother during the day after my adventures, and sitting on the couch in her den. There I would have conversations with her about everything that goes on in a young child's world. I'd watch her crochet and she often let me pick out one of her whatnots from the large display shelves that flanked the back of the den. These were whatnots that she had collected over the decades of travel, but they were treasures to me. There were steins from her time in Germany, brass figures from Spain, and porcelain characters like a rabbit eating corn that would play music when you wound up the dial at the bottom.

However, I was also very close to my grandfather on my mom's side. Within days of arriving, I knew this world would be different. Thurmond's world was structured, predictable, and everything moved with a rhythm. Dinner was always prepared and on the table at the same time. Beds were made, and everything had its place. I remember his work shed behind their home—his tools, while worn from years of use, were always hung or shelved exactly where they belonged. The air carried the scent of motor oil and transmission fluid—something old, but familiar.

Cooter's farm was alive with possibility. It was exciting—completely different. He had his own regiment of routines, for sure, but every day felt unpredictable. He seemed to roll with the winds of change. If he had a project in motion but a neighbor drove up, he'd quickly pivot. If rain rolled in, he'd hurry to feed the animals, then settle onto the front porch to read his Bible—or show me how to sharpen a knife.

Where my grandmother Mary's world was warm and nurturing, my grandmother Helen's world was much more rigid and echoed a life shaped by survival.

Having so many cousins nearby sweetened the deal, offering endless chances for play and adventure. For a ten-year-old boy, it was paradise. A few of those cousins lived right in the area of my grandparents' farm. Jesse was quite a bit older than I was and sometimes came across as a rebel. James and I were the same age and were close. But one cousin in particular made the move most exciting. My cousin Adam was now my new next-door neighbor. He was two years older, and our March birthdays were just five days apart. Like me, he was an only child. We were close from day one.

Adam had this way of making everything feel like an adventure—even if all we had were sticks and imagination. If I was ever sad or unsure, he always cracked a joke first, like laughter could beat back the clouds.

It had been normal for me to sleep over at my dad's parents' house, and I carried that tradition over. Adam and I quickly devised a system to spend as many nights together as possible. One night at his house, one at mine, then we'd each ask to sleep at our grandparents'—without letting on that we'd be meeting up there. Three nights, three locations. We thought we were geniuses.

But they were all in on it. One day, while visiting my grandmother to pick up vegetables, my uncle Renard (Adam's dad) dropped by. I overheard my name, then Adam's. My uncle chuckled and said, "Yeah, these boys think they're slick. They're determined to spend every night together if it kills 'em." Laughter echoed all around.

We had so many good times at my grandmother's house. I remember Easter Sundays—coming home from church to a huge meal and then hunting eggs to see who'd find the most. All of us would gather in the

28

side yard to play a few games of football, pretending to be Joe Montana and Jerry Rice.

One Sunday, it started like any other lazy Easter afternoon. The sun was warm, the scent of honeysuckle hung in the air, and our bellies were full from ham, biscuits, and too many deviled eggs.

We were all still buzzed from the egg hunt, pockets jingling with jelly beans and loose coins, when Jesse suggested we go exploring. He had that wild look in his eyes—part daredevil, part ringleader.

"Let's check the old barn," he said, already moving toward it without waiting for a response.

My grandmother said that her mother had told her she remembered Union soldiers tying their horses up to that barn when she was a child, during the Civil War on their way to take Savannah.

Adam and I hesitated, but curiosity always won.

Inside the barn, dust hung in the air like smoke, and the light streaming through the cracks in the siding made it feel like we were stepping into a dream—or a trap.

Jesse scaled the hay bales like a raccoon, laughing as he vanished behind a stack near the far wall. We heard rustling, then silence.

And then: SNAP!

A sound like bone meeting steel.

Jesse's scream followed. Not a cry. A howl. It tore through the barn and hit our chests like a hammer.

"HELP! It's got me!" he wailed.

Adam and I froze. I remember looking into his eyes and seeing my own fear reflected back at me.

Jesse's hand had landed in an old bear trap—set long ago by our grandfather to keep pests out. It had rusted in the shadows, forgotten until that moment.

"What do we do?!" I shouted.

"I—I don't know!" Adam said, his voice cracking.

31

Jesse kept screaming. His face was red, veins bulging, the trap biting deep into his palm. Blood dripped from his fingers onto the hay.

And that's when we bolted.

We ran. Out of the barn. Across the yard. Breath burning, legs pumping, guilt chasing us.

By the time our uncles got to Jesse, the damage had been done.

Later that night, as I lay awake, I realized something that's stuck with me ever since:

Even in paradise, danger lives in the corners left checked.

And even games can turn deadly when no one's watching.

Those days? Those were the good 'ol days.

Chapter 3:

OLD MAN & ME

My grandfather seemed to have legend status. Everywhere he went, he ran into someone he knew. He became my first mentor. After we settled in, I stuck to him like glue. He carried a quiet authority and a natural magnetism that drew people in. He had served as a sharpshooter in the Marines. And he was part of the first soldiers that stormed the beaches of Guadalcanal in WWII.

His life had been hard, but it molded him into a man of remarkable integrity. If you've ever seen the world-famous shooter Jerry Miculek, you'll have a pretty good idea of what my grandfather looked like— they favored each other closely.

He was the first person I ever knew who had his own unique sense of style and brand. Even though he was a farmer, he never left the house looking like he didn't care. He always wore a button-up shirt, sleeves rolled depending on the season—long sleeves in winter, short sleeves in summer. Most were some version of plaid. In his back pocket, he kept a handkerchief. He always carried a pocket watch and a small knife, no matter where he went. And he topped it all off with a trucker-style cap—the puffy kind with a flat brim, often bearing a random logo from a feed store or farm equipment company. Most of those hats were gifts, so brand loyalty had nothing to do with it.

He taught me the meaning of hard work, integrity, loyalty, and life itself. During the spring and summer, he'd wake me up early to go pick vegetables in the fields. Corn was my favorite—it was easy to judge and simple to harvest. If the ear was too small, you left it. If it was big enough, you snapped it off and dropped it in the bucket. Peas weren't terrible to pick, but the worst part came later, sitting on the porch shelling them. Corn was easier in that regard too; shucking was quicker. Peas, though—shelling them turned your thumbs raw. After cracking them open, you'd run the inside of your thumb along the seam to pop the peas out. It wouldn't take long before that tough outer shell wore your skin down and stained your fingers greenish-yellow from the hull.. Still, we did it. Because that's what had to be done.

My favorite to load, though the heaviest, was watermelon. We'd sometimes break one open right there in the field, and devour it right there. No silverware. No napkins. Just my grandfathers' pocket knife to cut a slice, juice running down our arms and smiles all around.

My grandfather was also a wizard around animals. He had a rhythm to his chores—feeding, watering, checking on every single creature with practiced efficiency. Nothing went to waste. The kitchen had its own rituals too. My grandmother was a wonderful cook, but the kitchen was also where my grandfather kept a small metal bucket for food scraps. If someone threw away leftovers and he found them in the trashcan, it would set him off. Those scraps weren't trash—they were feed for the hogs. And if he was in the house, we weren't allowed to use the microwave. He had a pacemaker, and back then, we were told that microwaves could interfere with the batteries. So, we adapted and did as we were asked.

He loved his animals like they were family. I remember him having me hold a chicken once—sick and flapping—while he applied a strange purple medicine to its head. He called it "medicurracaine." I'm still not sure if that was its real name or just something he made up. Either way, it worked.

He taught me there was a world of difference between just having animals and knowing them.

He'd say "Robbie! Come over here and let me learn you something."

Chickens weren't just chickens—there were game hens, silkies, bantams. And they all had their own personalities and you had to treat them accordingly.

He had guineas, turkeys, peacocks. Pigs, cows, rabbits, quail. And he knew exactly how to care for each one. His knowledge was encyclopedic, but never boastful. He simply lived it.

He also kept honeybees. I could tell they were one of his favorite things. He must've had at least a dozen hives scattered across the property. I'd often see him grab his smoker—a small metal container with a funnel-shaped top, attached to a hand-pump that looked like an old organ bellows. He'd pack it with dried pine straw, light it, and wait for smoke to start drifting from the spout. Then he'd begin pressing the pump, letting thin streams of smoke swirl around the top of each hive before slowly cracking the lid open.

Most of the time, he didn't wear any protective clothing. He knew his bees. He could sense when it was safe to poke around and when it was time to suit up. At first, I was scared—I didn't want to get stung. I hadn't been on the farm long, but I'd already had a few run-ins with wasps and yellow jackets while out playing, not knowing I needed to pay more attention to my surroundings.

Watching him work with the bees and tend to the needs of his animals taught me that nature had its own language—one he understood without words. And little by little, I began to listen too.

People often pulled into the yard looking to buy something—maybe just a chicken—but he always used the opportunity to show off the whole farm. Not to brag, but because he was proud. He knew how to sell without even knowing what the term "marketing" meant.

He created moments. He made people want to buy more than they came for. I didn't realize it at the time, but I was learning things like tactics, storytelling, and customer service from a man who never used those words.

The front porch of the farmhouse was wide, about five feet off the ground, stretching across the entire front of the house. On the far-right side was his rocking chair. There were many chairs out there on the porch, but that one was his. It was painted gray, its finish cracking from years of sun and seasons—a quiet witness to everything that passed before it. It was adjacent to the barn and the animals and caught the sunrise just behind his left shoulder. That's where we had our talks—where I learned the most important lessons.

Most late mornings started the same way: a cup of coffee in his hand, a Bible in his lap, and a quiet reverence in the air that made even the wind seem to whisper. I'd sit beside him, legs swinging off the edge of a rocking chair, pretending not to watch as he ran his finger across a passage. I was just starting my day, but he had been up for hours tending to his flock.

He didn't read to impress. He read to remind himself of something. Sometimes he'd nod quietly, sometimes he'd hum a hymn under his breath. That porch wasn't just where we sat—it was his sanctuary. And over time, it taught me the importance of having a special place that would bring you back to what's important.

"Always start your day with God," he told me once, tapping his Bible. "He'll guide you better than any compass ever will."

"Robbie, you are so lucky. You've got your whole life ahead of you," he'd say. "There's a scary world out there, and I pray you never have to see the things I've seen. But no matter what, always remember—God has a plan, and He has a purpose for your life. Be thankful.

You better always be thankful. There's many people out there who have it so much worse."

And then he'd start thanking God right there on the porch. For the animals, the rain, the food, the family. He never had much, but his gratitude list was always long. Whether intentional or not, he was teaching me right there in the moment, how to do just that.

"One day at a time, sweet Jesus," he'd whisper like a prayer, sometimes out loud, sometimes just to himself. It was his reset button—his way of surrendering control and trusting that tomorrow would take care of itself.

I didn't understand the weight of that phrase back then. But later in life, when I'd find myself overwhelmed by work, by grief, or by everything in between—I'd catch myself whispering it too.

Not because I needed a cliché. But because I needed his strength. His peace. His way.

I didn't know it then, but I learned later that Cooter had battled alcoholism in his younger days. He'd made mistakes and hurt people. He had once lived on the wrong side of life. But the man I knew had turned it all around. He was a churchgoer, a helper, a pillar of the community—beloved and relied upon by everyone.

He had two vehicles. His old red Ford F100 work truck—a long bed, a few dents, a true workhorse. The second was the ugliest car I'd ever seen: a brown Ford Granada, with just enough yellow tint to earn the nickname I gave it—the "vomit-mobile." It might have been ugly, but it ran. It got us to church every Sunday and took him to the doctor when needed. That car had a role, and it did it well.

Among his eight grandchildren, I was the second youngest but the only one he truly trusted with special responsibilities. Every Friday evening before sundown, he'd load up animals in the back of his truck for the Saturday flea market trip. I rarely saw him take any of my cousins. But he took me, again and again. Eventually, he even trusted me to run the stall while he stepped away to look around, and grab us lunch. I remember the first time I sold a few chickens while he was gone. I'd memorized the prices but devised my strategy of asking a bit more—and I got it. Exceeding his expectations felt incredible. He told that story for months.

We lost him in the year 2000, about three years after I had lost my grandfather Thurmond in a tragic accident. That funeral—his funeral—was the hardest day of my life up to that point. Saying goodbye to my hero, my rock, my mentor, crushed me. It shook the foundation I had been standing on.

But life, as he taught me, carries on. It doesn't stop for grief. It doesn't pause for heartbreak. And we have to decide—will we carry the wisdom, the love, the memories, and use them to grow? Will we roll with the wind, as he had done for many decades? Or will we let them drift away like the many sunsets I watched from that front porch with him, as they faded beyond the trees?

He didn't leave behind riches or a big inheritance. But what he gave me was far more valuable: a blueprint. A set of values. A deep understanding that character matters, that hard work pays off, and that faith is something to hold onto even when the rest of the world doesn't make sense.

The old man is gone, but he's still with me. In the choices I make. In the way I live my life. In the way I pray.

I didn't know it at the time, but I was being shaped every day—by his quiet consistency, his moral compass, his way of letting God steer even when the road got rough. In the leadership meetings I'd one day enter, in the quiet moments I'd spend fathering my own children, and in the values I've fought to hold onto—I can trace the thread back to that porch. To him.

Years later, before big meetings or on hard days, I still find myself reaching for that quiet clarity I saw in him. I'll pause, take a deep breath, and remember him rocking slowly on that porch, whispering prayers into the fading light.

And every now and then, when I see a sunrise peeking over my left shoulder, I swear I can still hear his voice reminding me a phrase I heard him say so many times—One day at a time, sweet Jesus. One day at a time.

Chapter 4:

CHEMICALS BETWEEN US

My grandfather had become my first mentor. But Adam was my first confidant. Even before our move, I always looked forward to playing with him whenever my mother would take me over to my grandparents' farm.

There was a long dirt path that separated my grandparents' house from Adam's, flanked by tall pines, oaks and pecan trees, along with occasional thick patches of wild blackberry bushes. That path might as well have been the yellow brick road. The moment I saw Adam standing in the yard—stick in hand—I knew adventure awaited. Whether it was sword fighting with branches, trying to catch crawfish in ditches, or pretending we were Braves players warming up for a big game, we threw ourselves into each day like it was our last.

We were kindred spirits. Out of all our cousins, we were the only two who didn't have siblings. And it didn't take long before we considered each other brothers.

Sometimes we'd talk about how cool it would be to be real brothers. And when either of us got in trouble at home, we'd think to ourselves conspiratorially, "Just wait till I'm old enough to move out someday—we'll have our own place and play video games all night." That fantasy, far-fetched as it was, carried us through more than one tough week. And ultimately, that dream became reality in 2002.

Our bond grew quickly—like a wildfire during a drought-stricken summer. When life felt too big to handle or too hard to understand, Adam was a trustworthy and wise sounding board.

There was one evening—I must've been around twelve—when my parents got into a huge fight. I don't remember what it was about, but I do remember sneaking out the front door and walking the short distance to Adam's house. I knocked on the door and when he opened it, I just said "they're fighting again". He didn't ask questions. He just handed me the extra controller, and we played Mario Kart until I forgot how upset I was. That was Adam. He didn't need to fix things. He just made sure I never had to face anything alone.

I didn't understand it then, but my mother was unraveling. Some mornings she was fine, almost normal. Other days she wouldn't get out of bed, wouldn't eat, wouldn't speak. Her mood could shift like lightning—one moment humming Pink Floyd while stirring sweet tea, the next, slamming cabinet doors so hard the dishes rattled, screaming about a fork being in the wrong drawer.

My earliest understanding of mental illness came during a quiet conversation with Adam. Our Uncle Don—my mom's youngest brother—still lived at home with my grandparents. I always knew he was different. I just didn't understand why. He never said much to anyone. He rarely stepped outside of the house either.

One day, I asked Adam what was wrong with Uncle Don—why he never left the house, why he barely spoke, why he always seemed to be somewhere else, even when he was right in front of you.

Adam said he had heard it all started back when Don was in high school. Don had been in line to receive a big award—something important. But at the last moment, it was taken away after someone realized there had been a mistake. Adam said Don felt

52

humiliated, like the rug had been pulled out from under him. And after that, something changed. Something snapped. He was never the same again.

Adam was gifted with book smarts. He was always extremely intelligent for his age. Eventually, he became valedictorian of his class, graduated from Georgia Tech and went on to become an engineer for the Corps. I always wondered how he'd become so smart. I was the exact opposite—a solid C student who hated sitting in class. But the truth was, Adam put in the time. He did the work to grow and achieve. He embraced learning.

He also put in the time to be a great friend. Adam was two years older than I was. Being only two years apart meant we shared a lot of the same interests— from our love for the Atlanta Braves and Falcons, to SportsCenter, Mario Kart, and, most importantly, anything that could be done outdoors.

Our grandmother would babysit Adam during the week while his mother, Joyce, worked at an office. And every morning, the first thing I'd do was rush out the door and run over to my grandparents' house, ready to embrace another day of play with him.

When we weren't together, we'd drive our parents crazy by sitting on the phone for hours, talking about whatever we were watching on TV or what we planned to do the next day. There were no cell phones back then, so being on the landline meant no one else could get through.

It wasn't always sunshine and smooth sailing. Boys will be boys, and every now and then one of us would get bent out of shape and start a fight. He was short for his age, so we were very similar in height. And I always had the mindset that since we were similar in staure, it didn't matter that he was older—I could take him. We'd lock up, start wrestling, and inevitably I'd end up in a headlock, tapping out. Sometimes I thought I was getting the best of him, but he always endured and overcame. He was tough as a bull for someone his size.

However, those moments of sibling-like rivalry were few and far between. Through it all, I knew I could always count on Adam to have my back.

One of those early summers together we developed a gameplan. I had been complaining to him about my parents' drug usage and how it bothered me. They had been growing a giant marijuana plant in a large gray pot behind the fence in our backyard.

It wasn't just the pot in the backyard—it was the pills, the alcohol, the silence. They formed an invisible barrier, like a fog that thickened until I couldn't even see the mother I remembered.

The chemicals between us weren't just the ones growing behind the fence. They were the unspoken things, the glances I didn't understand, the walls that went up every time I tried to talk to her, her mental state. We were living in a haze, and Adam was the only one who helped me see through it.

Adam had an ingenious plan. He remembered that I'd gotten a chemistry set the previous Christmas—complete with about thirty small vials of powders and liquids designed to create all kinds of reactions. He said some of those vials contained substances that might be toxic to plants.

So, we decided to camp out in the backyard one evening, bringing the chemistry set with us. We stayed up late that night until we saw the lights inside the trailer turn off. That's when we went to work. We called it "Operation Meltdown." We had no idea if it would work, but we felt like undercover agents. On a mission to save the world! We used my old army surplus canteen to mix the chemicals and whispered like we were being tailed by enemy spies. Every crunch of a pinecone or rustle in the grass made us jump. It was the kind of mission you only take on if you believe—fiercely—in justice, and in each other. We had already staged a small bucket of water nearby. All we had to do was add the mixture Adam concocted and pour it over the plant, letting the soil soak it in.

After the mission was complete, we climbed into our sleeping bags and talked about sports until we both fell asleep.

The next morning, when the sun came up, we stretched and wiped the sleep from our eyes. We unzipped the tent with eager anticipation, hoping to see a dead plant. Sadly, it looked no different than it had the day before. Nothing had happened.

We cleaned up, packed our things, and went about our day—disappointed. We thought we had failed our mission.

That night, back inside the trailer, my mom barely spoke. She sat in the living room with the lights off, the glow of the TV flickering shadows onto the hallway wall. It didn't feel like a victory yet—it felt like waiting for the storm to pass. Even when I'd won a battle, I still lived in a warzone.

A few days later, much to my surprise, I was playing in the backyard when I noticed the plant was drooping and turning brown.

I couldn't believe it. I remember walking up to it slowly, like it might spring back to life at any second. But no—its leaves were curled, and the rich green had turned brittle and gray. That plant was toast. I laughed. Not just a giggle—a belly laugh. A release. That was the first time I remember feeling like I had some power over my environment. That Adam and I, together, had done something that mattered—even if no one else would ever understand why.

When that plant finally drooped, it wasn't just a science experiment gone right. It felt like I had reclaimed something. Like maybe—just maybe—I had the power to fight back against the things that were poisoning my life. And for once, I wasn't powerless.

That plant wasn't just weed—it was every broken promise, every night I sat alone in my room, every angry whisper behind closed doors. Watching it wilt felt like finally pushing back against the chaos.

"We did it!" I shouted.

Had anyone been around to hear me, they probably would've thought I was crazy—shouting into the air, grinning like a madman. I immediately took off running to Adam's house to give him the good news.

That week, I walked a little taller—like I'd taken back something that was stolen from me. Adam and I didn't talk much about what it meant, but I could tell he felt it too. Sometimes, the smallest victories mean everything when you've got so little control over your world.

A few days later, I saw my parents standing next to the plant having a conversation. Shortly afterward, they pulled it up by the roots and cast it aside.

It was an amazing feeling—putting together a plan, executing it, and seeing it succeed. For the first time, I felt powerful.

Adam and I went on to have many adventures through the years. And just like those early days, we always had each other's backs. Unfortunately, sometimes that mindset ended up being costly.

One day, riding home from school in the passenger seat of Adam's truck we got into an accident. He had a mid-'90s Ford Ranger. It was a small, manual transmission truck—Ford blue—but a great ride. His father had bought it brand new for him when he turned 16. On this particular day, we were taking the back roads home, and Adam was having a little fun downshifting around a corner, watching the dirt fly up behind us. That's when he began to drift and slid into the ditch.

We had to walk about a mile to the next driveway, and luckily the owner—an old farmer—was home. He gladly brought his tractor down and pulled us out.

The accident, which only left a small dent in the side of the truck, was fixed in about five minutes. But we were about an hour or so, late getting home.

This is where most people might expect a stern talking-to from Adam's parents. But that's not what happened. Instead, I was the one who got grounded— for two weeks. My parents accused me of being the one at fault. They were worried when we hadn't showed up at our normal time. And while they were glad that we were okay, they said I was probably the reason he wrecked.

The next morning, when Adam picked me up for school, he told me his parents had simply said, "Be more careful next time," and that was that.

That moment stuck with me. Not because of what they said—but because of what they didn't. There was no blame. No lecture. Just trust. Adam's parents trusted him—and by extension, they trusted me. And that trust felt like a kind of forgiveness I hadn't known I needed. When I sat in his truck that morning, I didn't feel like the kid who always got blamed anymore. I felt like someone who deserved a second chance. I realized then that the way adults respond to your mistakes teaches you something about who you are—or at least who they think you are. My parents assumed I was reckless, a bad influence. Adam's parents assumed he just made a mistake. One saw danger; the other saw growing up.

It wasn't the last time I learned that some people just believe in you more than others. And Adam, no matter what, never stopped believing in me. Looking back now, I think everyone needs an Adam in their life. A family member who shows up when the rest of your world is unraveling. Someone who doesn't need to save you, but who makes you feel worth saving. He was my first glimpse of what loyalty without judgment looked like—and I carried that lesson with me into every real friendship I formed after.

Chapter 5:

YOU DON'T KNOW HOW IT FEELS

My grade school years were anything but ordinary. In a town where most kids cared more about tractors than textbooks, I was trying to survive more than just spelling tests. I started out in public school like the vast majority of other children in Ellabell. There, most families were either poor or dirt poor. This was a town with no traffic light—just a few small fueling stations, a post office, and a very small independent grocery store. Life was different back then—the biggest thing you had to worry about was getting into a fistfight with someone. And that was usually over a girl.

THE DIRT ROAD

In kindergarten, I had one of my first big adventures. My school was a small bright red schoolhouse on the corner—the same one both my parents had attended years before.

The years had passed, the building had aged, but kids were still being kids. One day, a group of my classmates had surrounded a baby squirrel, and I decided it'd be a great idea to jump in the middle and catch it. So, I did. It's one of those vivid memories that takes me back every time I think of it. I still don't know how I made it more than one step before the squirrel bit me right on the finger, but somehow, I did—a hard lesson learned. I had to get a shot that day. While I don't remember the pain from the shot or even getting it, I do remember sitting in the classroom by myself, watching my classmates play outside while I waited for my mom to pick me up.

Back home, I had become a legend in my own mind. My father, grandfather, and grandmother chuckled and swapped stories about how brave I was at five years old to capture that squirrel with my bare hands. My mother, always a bit overprotective, wasn't amused—she was convinced I might die from some disease. Unfortunately, the kids at school had heard the wild scream I let out when it bit me, and they saw the tears that ran down my face as I ran to the teacher, screaming for help. I had been brave, but I hadn't been tough. Nonetheless, it had established myself as a player within the social dynamics of our childhood kindergarten ecosystems.

Those early years were fantastic. I had started playing baseball a year prior, in my preschool year—a sport that would stick with me all the way through graduating high school. Baseball was my life. I lived, breathed, and slept baseball. From collecting baseball cards, to watching games on TV, to going to the occasional minor league game to see the Savannah Cardinals, now known as the Banana's—it was everything to me. I remember riding in the backseat of the car on our way to my games. "Life is a highway" was a popular hit that would often come on. And every time I felt pumped by the lyrics and the melody. If you asked me what I wanted to be when I grew up, I wouldn't have hesitated to tell you: a Major League Baseball player. Being the next Indiana Jones was a distant second.

For all their struggles with addiction, my parents were always supportive of me playing ball. Every year, they signed me up, paid for uniforms, took me to practices, and showed up to games. They proudly displayed my trophies in the living room, adding to the collection year after year. They loved it. And I loved it too. From pretending to hit the game-winning home run in the front yard, to playing catch with my dad, to lying on my bed blowing bubbles with my gum while he laced up my cleats before a game—baseball life felt perfect.

But not long after we moved, the decision was made that I should switch to private school. I'm almost certain the idea came from my grandparents. They had always talked about Pinewood like it was the promised land. Their second son—my Uncle Royce—had gone to Pinewood Christian Academy, about thirty minutes north of where we lived. Somehow, a poor kid living in a trailer ended up making that same transition.

At first, I was actually a little excited. I remembered seeing the photos of my Uncle Royce in his football jersey at my grandparents' house and seeing his trophies. I had overheard my grandmother talking about Pinewood several times over the years and how great of a school it was. I wondered if I would meet friends that were just as passionate about baseball as I was, or if maybe I would play football like my uncle. Ultimately, I spent sixth through eighth grade there— and I hated every minute of it.

It wasn't the school itself or the long bus rides—it was the people. My classmates all came from wealthy families. The teachers and faculty were well off. But me? I stuck out like a sore thumb. Backwoods. Country-bumpkin. Redneck. And kids that age can be brutal.

Going to Pinewood meant my mother was no longer taking me to school. Now I was waiting for the bus at the end of the dirt road, just like my cousins. The bus for Pinewood always arrived first since it had a longer distance to travel.

The bus would wheeze and cough to a stop, and I would climb in, the scent of diesel and vinyl wrapping around me like a second skin. The seats had two large green vinyl cushions that were firm, with one for the seat and one for the back. I can remember them being ice cold in the winter months and scorching hot on your legs while wearing shorts those first and last months of the school year.

The hallways at Pinewood smelled like lemon cleaner and new carpet, with portraits of past headmasters lining the walls like royalty. It wasn't just the uniforms and the shiny floors—it was a whole other world, and I didn't speak the language.

I managed to make a few friends, but by that time, the pressures of home life were starting to affect me. This was around the age boys start noticing girls differently and I had a crush on the prettiest girl in my grade—Myra. I didn't stand a chance, between my confidence issues from never quite fitting in and the stress from home. I had gone from being a skinny kid to getting a little chubby, and that hit my self-confidence hard. Still, that didn't stop me from dreaming. That first year I asked my mom if I could pick up a Valentines Day gift for her. She took me to the store and helped me pick out a tiny heart shaped box filled with a few pieces of chocolate. The next day I awkwardly approached her and gave it to her. She thanked me kindly—sweetly, even—but never hinted at anything more. And I knew what that meant. At that point I realized, I may be able to hit a fastball, but on that day when it came to my big opportunity, I struck out.

I didn't blame her. Not really. But for the first time, I started to understand what it meant to not be enough—not smart enough, not rich enough, not cool enough. It stuck to me like dust from the dirt road, and no matter how hard I tried, I couldn't shake it off.

Unfortunately, the grade's biggest bully, Drew— who was three times my size and did play football— had other plans for my tenure at Pinewood. For three years, I focused on survival. Drew threatened me

71

constantly. Always making hateful comments, pushing me when teachers weren't looking, whispering threats in the hallway, knocking over my books, and warning he'd beat me to a pulp if he ever caught me alone.

I hadn't done anything wrong to get on Drew's radar. It was simply because he knew I wasn't like them. They all had Bugle Boy and Ralph Lauren polo shirts. They wore Jams shorts. And there I was in my brand-new Reebok Pumps that my grandmother had purchased for me, and the cheapest generic solid-color polo shirt that bore no logo, my mother could find. I hated being judged because my clothes didn't meet their standard. Back at home, I barely wore a shirt half the time.

I kept my head on a swivel and the constant fear of being pummeled wore on me. In class I would sit, scribbling tiny stars on my notebook over and over again. The kind where you don't pick your pencil up. Just five tiny lines, one after the other. A pentagram. I remember sitting on the bus ride home, staring out the window, dreading the next day before the current one had even ended...

Keep in mind, I wasn't a perfect student. I was a prankster—and I got that honest from my father. He was always telling stories about the tricks he'd pulled on guys he worked with over the years. One of his favorites was about putting a large ball bearing, about the size of a golfball, inside an empty toolbox in the back of a work truck right before a coworker headed to a job site in downtown Savannah. He'd bend over in laughter describing the clunk of metal rolling with every turn, echoing down city streets, while his co-worker was stuck in traffic. Another time, he opened the toolbox on a golf cart just enough so that when someone drove off, the tools spilled out onto the gravel behind them. He thought that was comedy gold.

And just like that, I started finding small ways to get a laugh—little pranks that gave me a moment of joy in days that often felt heavy. I'd unzip a backpack so it would spill open when someone picked it up. Or sneak a "kick me" sign onto a classmate's back. At the time, I saw it as harmless fun—me pushing back against the world that pushed so hard on me. But looking back, I cringe. Those moments, innocent as they seemed, were really about rebellion. I had been

73

bullied, and part of me was trying to flip the script—even if it was only in jest.

But I always had a good heart. The lessons from both of my grandfather's ran deep. I never got into drugs. I didn't run with the wrong crowd. I had lines I wouldn't cross. Unfortunately, the principal at Pinewood didn't know any of that.

One day in the restroom, I used a stall—always did. It felt safer than the urinals on the wall. Apparently, someone before me had been smoking. I saw the cigarette butt floating in the bowl when I walked in. I didn't bother flushing it. I didn't even think twice about it. I did my business, flushed the toilet, and thought nothing of it—until I heard a loud banging on the door.

It was the principal—Mr. Wells.

Mr. Wells was known as an enforcer. He didn't just uphold the rules—he lived for them. Inside his office hung a large wooden paddle, about two feet long, with nine quarter-sized holes drilled straight through. Everyone at Pinewood knew the legend: the holes were there to make it hurt more, to reduce wind resistance, to sting. Whether or not anyone had actually been swatted with it didn't matter. The rumor was enough. Mr. Wells kept the paddle up like a badge of honor—a silent warning for every student who crossed his threshold. Some kids swore they'd heard it crack against a desk when someone mouthed off. Others claimed the holes weren't just for sting, but for speed—to cut through the air quicker. Whether any of it was true didn't matter. The myth had already done its job. Just seeing it made your stomach twist.

He barged in as soon as I unlocked the door, certain he'd caught me in the act. I denied it immediately, but I've never forgotten the feeling I had when he grabbed my hands and said, "You're lying— your fingernails are yellow." I was just a kid. I didn't know whether yellow fingernails really meant anything or if he was just looking for a reason to judge me. The decolorization was from farm life. But in my mind, he was saying between the lines: You're just a piece of white trash.

When he grabbed my hands and looked at my nails, I didn't just feel accused—I felt exposed. Like everything I'd ever tried to hide about who I was had been dragged into the light. I wanted to disappear into the floor. I wanted someone—anyone—to believe me without asking for proof.

It crushed me. It didn't matter what I did, what I didn't do, or how hard I tried. People had already decided who I was. But I knew better—I wasn't the kid they saw. I just didn't know how to show them yet.

He dragged me to the office, called my parents, and left me pleading—trying to convince them I wasn't like them. That I hadn't been smoking. That I never would. That I wasn't like them.

It took time, but they eventually believed me. I think at first, they assumed I must have been smoking because they both smoked—and had for as long as I could remember. Maybe they thought they had been a bad influence.

But this was the first time I pushed back sharply. I told them I didn't want to be like them. I didn't want to smoke. I didn't want to do drugs. I didn't want to follow the same path. I wanted more. I wanted different. I wanted to be me.

Saying it out loud scared me—more than anything else ever had. What if they were hurt? What if they didn't care? But for once, I didn't back down. I needed them to hear it. I needed to hear myself say it.

I think the confession of my true feelings caught them off guard. And I think it stung them, much like the paddle in Mr. Well's office was rumored to do.

They paused, reflected, and agreed. I didn't need to be like them. I could be better.

That night, I pulled the covers over my head and stared into the dark, wondering why the world seemed so determined to see me as someone I wasn't. Tom Petty's words played over in my mind—"You don't know how it feels... to be me."

It was a far cry from the days I used to blast Life is a Highway, dreaming of adventure and life like an open road. That carefree spirit felt miles away now.

I made it through the rest of my middle school years at Pinewood by keeping my head down and my heart guarded. I became a ghost in the hallways as best as I could—quiet, careful, always just out of Drew's line of sight. Each day, I sat in that classroom like a clock with no hands, waiting for the bell to break the silence. Not for the promise of learning, but for release—for the chance to run. Back to the farm. Back to Adam. Back to baseball. Back to anywhere that felt like freedom. Anywhere that reminded me who I really was.

Chapter 6:

SOLITUDE

What I'm about to tell you is an embarrassing story. It's about a time when Adam and I did something pretty shameful—something I'm certainly not proud of. I previously mentioned that I was a bit mischievous. That I was a prankster. I had a good soul and good intentions, but I never missed an opportunity to humor myself at someone else's expense. And those are actions that I'm not proud of today.

In our small town of Ellabell, there was a man named Ricky who lived down the road from my grandparents' house. He was an older, handicapped

81

gentleman. He loved to talk, and he was a good man, but at our age, we saw him as a bit of an annoyance. He spoke slowly, with a long, drawn-out Southern accent. At his core, he was just a lonely old man. Every so often, he would come over and chat with my grandmother on the front porch.

For the most-part our grandmother enjoyed his company and their conversations. Grandma Helen never said an ill word about Ricky. As a Christian, she genuinely cared about him, but sometimes she wasn't in the mood to sit and talk for hours on end.

One summer day, we heard his crutches clink as he muscled his way down the long dirt road and up the clay hill where their home sat. Grandma Helen rolled her eyes in annoyance that day. She muttered something under her breath, loud enough for us to hear—something like, "Oh Lord, here comes Ricky again."

SOLITUDE

That day, Adam and I devised a plan.

We had developed a habit of picking pears from my grandparents' yard and throwing them at things we shouldn't. Like the cows, or onto the barn— sometimes even onto my grandmother's house when no one was around. Both buildings had tin roofs. As kids, it was pretty entertaining to launch the pears as high as we could throw them, wait for the impact to come crashing down, and then listen to the thumps as the oblong shaped fruit rolled down the steep-angled roofs.

That Friday night, while everyone was asleep, we decided to sneak out and terrorize Ricky. Like ghosts in the night, we would sneak in, create turmoil, and disappear—leaving him wondering what had happened.

As we often spent the night at each other's houses and stayed up playing video games late into the early morning hours, It worked out perfectly for our plan. More often than not, we stayed at Adam's because he had nicer toys and more up-to-date Super Nintendo games. It was also easier to sneak out of his house because he lived in a double-wide trailer, with more distance between his parents' room and the back door.

It was probably two or three o'clock in the morning when we snuck out. The summer night sky, star-filled and glowing in a soft grayish-blue hue, made it easy to navigate. We were ready to execute.

We quietly made our way down the long dirt road. We had pre-staged a stack of pears next to the giant oak tree that marked the entrance to the dirt road leading to our houses and our grandparents' driveway on the other side. That oak was ancient, a titan of the land—so wide that five grown men couldn't encircle it arm to arm."

As we passed, a thought crossed my mind: I wonder how many rebellious acts this oak tree has seen over the many decades of its existence.

Ricky's house was also on a dirt road directly across the main street from ours.

Ready for action, our weapons of choice were in hand: two "hand grenade bombs" falling from the clear night sky as high as we could launch them. We knew the higher we threw, the harder the pears would hit.

And just like that—they did.

We heaved one pear after another into the air. Bam! Bam! They started hitting his tin roof—clank,

clank—as they rolled down and finished with a deep plunk when they hit the ground.

It didn't take long for the porch light to flick on. Ricky popped out the front door yelling, "Y'all bunch of hoodlums, get on out of here before I call the law!" And off we ran.

Our stomachs hurt from the bouts of laughter. Our message had been delivered! We had accomplished our mission. Unscathed. Thankfully, no shots fired. It felt priceless.

Until it didn't.

The next morning, Uncle Renard woke us up. We had fallen asleep on Adam's bedroom floor, exhausted from our late-night escapades.

"Hey boys, y'all get on up. You got somebody here to see you," Renard said.

I didn't think anything of it—I assumed it was Jesse coming to hang out for the day. Tired, we wiped the sleep from our eyes, slowly got up, and made our way to the living room.

I'll never forget the feeling I got as I turned the corner. It felt like the back of my throat dropped into the pit of my stomach.

The first thing I saw was my father. And I knew exactly what that meant.

The second thing I saw was a uniform and a police badge.

87

My heart began to race. My whole body felt like it was going through some kind of metamorphosis.

The jig was up. Just like that, we were caught.

The walk down the dirt road with my dad, the officer, and my uncle that morning seemed to take five times longer than the route we'd taken just hours before. It was the same route, though. This was confirmed pretty clearly by our footprints in the sand.

At this point, we were still denying the accusations.

Finally, as we stood in Ricky's front yard and continued to be pressed, I gave in. I folded.

"It was me. I did it," I said.

Adam immediately turned and looked at me with an annoyed, frustrated, and disappointed kind of look only an older sibling could make. He kept denying it!

The conversation between our dads and the officer shifted to what the punishment should be.

It seemed like they started enjoying it a little, at this point.

They quickly came to the decision that we would both face the wrath of our fathers back at home—and be required to cut Ricky's entire property with push mowers.

I was used to cutting grass with push mowers. There weren't self-propelled mowers back in those days. It was all manpower and sweat equity—I was responsible for mowing our acre of property every week—so the task itself wasn't too bad. In theory.

The problem was, it didn't look like Ricky had cut his yard that year. I started to wonder if he had ever cut it. The grass was almost as tall as we were.

Nonetheless, we gassed up the mowers and got to work.

Adam was still pretty upset with me for caving in and confessing. His face looked mad as a hornet the entire time it took us to finish cutting Ricky's yard.

Being he was so intelligent; he figured the footprints were only circumstantial evidence. Sure, it was obvious it was us, but there weren't any cameras in those days. If we had kept denying it and never admitted to it, at least we would've maintained some seed of doubt.

I, on the other hand, just wanted to get it over with. I had my fun. Now it was time to pay the piper.

I knew my parents—they made mountains out of molehills.

The brilliant idea of teenage terrorism that Adam and I had devised certainly would be considered more than a small hill. And it would likely be made into Mount Everest.

What had started as a prank wrapped in laughter ended with consequences that felt a hundred pounds heavier than the pears we'd thrown.

By the time we finished cutting Ricky's lawn, it seemed like it had been a long day already—even though it was still mid-morning.

We pushed the lawn mowers back home, put them away, and went our separate ways to face what was next. I knew mine would be worse. I just didn't realize how extreme it would end up being.

As soon as I walked in, I noticed my father sitting in his recliner.

Beer in hand. Stern look on his face.

"You think you're pretty smart, huh?" he asked in an angry, sarcastic tone.

"We'll see how smart you are now," he said as he walked over.

I knew I was about to get spanked.

My father had grown up getting a belt for discipline, and he made sure to pass the practice down to me.

But this time was worse. Much worse.

I was met with the full force of his right palm to my face. The very first of a small handful of times I'd end up taking a strike to the face from my father as a young adolescent.

The strike was jarring. It hurt. It knocked me to the ground.

"Get your ass up!" he said as tears streamed down my cheeks.

I tried apologizing frantically—even more so than I had earlier that morning at Ricky's after confessing.

But it was futile.

He took off his belt, grabbed my arm so I couldn't escape, and laid a series of lashes, one after another, until he felt like I had paid my due.

As his belt connected, time seemed to stall. The television froze mid-frame. The beer can wobbled in slow motion on the table as it was bumped. I saw the veins in his neck, the deep crease in his brow. And in that moment, I wasn't a boy who had made a mistake. I was a boy being made into someone else—someone who would carry this moment forever.

For most kids, this would've been the end.

The mercy rule. Finito.

But for me, this was only the end of the physical pain.

The mental price had yet to be paid.

I wasn't just ashamed of what I'd done. I was ashamed of who I had become in that moment. The sound of the belt wasn't the worst part—it was the sound of Ricky's voice echoing in my head, asking what kind of boys would throw pain at a man who had already known so much of it. I started to wonder if I was becoming the kind of person my grandparents wouldn't be proud of. That day, I lost more than my freedom—I lost a little of my innocence.

"Go to your room! You're grounded for the rest of the summer. You won't go outside! You won't watch TV! You won't play video games! You won't leave your room! Your ability to do anything for the rest of the summer will be based on what I tell you. Do you understand me?"

And he meant it.

I spent the vast majority of the next two months locked in my small 10'x9' room.

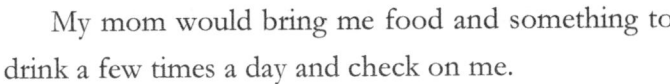

My mom would bring me food and something to drink a few times a day and check on me.

But together, they kept their word.

Nothing but the room.

It was a long summer.

I still had basic toys to keep me busy—action figures and comic books.

I studied the imperfections in the ceiling, the spider webs in the upper corners, the small channels in the paneling that lined the room.

THE DIRT ROAD

The window in my room became my television.

Unfortunately, the most eventful my view ever got was the birds passing by, a rabbit or two, or an occasional afternoon summer thunderstorm.

I spent many days thinking long and hard about my actions.

I wondered what my other cousins were up to. What my friends were doing.

About consequences.

About life.

Funny enough, I found myself doing push-ups and sit-ups—not realizing that's what most inmates in real prison cells do as well.

While I had been stripped of my creature comforts, I had managed to save a small Walkman that my parents missed when they surveyed my room for restricted items. It wasn't anything special—just an old gray-and-black recorder, big buttons on the side, and a turn dial for the volume and tuning radio stations.

I kept it tucked between my mattresses.

I had two small twin beds pushed together to make a larger bed, and it made a perfect place for a juvenile inmate to stash prized contraband.

This Walkman, though small, became the most valuable asset in my possession—an absolute lifesaver for enduring my sentence.

That little Walkman wasn't just contraband—it was my escape hatch, my tutor, my tether to the outside world. In the same four walls where I was expected to break, I was quietly building the mind of a thinker.

Every night, once I heard my parents close their door for bed, I would turn it on and scroll through the channels.

My parents often listened to music during the day, so I had that to carry me through.

But with the Walkman, I discovered late-night AM talk radio, and I quickly became hooked. Each night as I began to doze off, I'd press the record button and tuck it back into its hiding spot. The recordings gave me something to listen to on occasion when my mom would step out from time to time. I made sure to never get caught.

George H.W. Bush was president, and listening to news segments about his political decisions—and deep dives into his opposition with Bill Clinton and Ross Perot—became enamoring.

As a 12-year-old poor country boy, I was certainly not the target demographic the station had in mind.

It was surreal, really—me, a scrawny kid from a trailer in rural Georgia, listening to debates about national healthcare, foreign policy, and tax reform. I didn't understand every word, but I understood the stakes. These were grown men arguing about what kind of country we wanted to be. And for the first time, I began asking myself what kind of man I wanted to be. That Walkman planted the seed: that leadership mattered, that choices mattered, and that even a poor kid like me might someday have a voice.

That was the moment I fell in love with American politics.

But that was also when I started thinking differently about right and wrong—not just in the sense of rules, but in terms of impact. Of what it meant to hurt someone, to laugh at someone's expense. I began to develop something deeper than guilt: a conscience.

Looking back on that time, I realize the harm it caused to my psychological development.

By twelve years old, most children's minds have developed quite a bit, but they continue developing into their late teens and early twenties.

That time period forced me to rebuild my mental state and etched a scar on my personality that I've lived with ever since.

Still to this day, solitude feels like a familiar forge—where pain and stillness once melted me down and reshaped me. What started as punishment became practice. I learned to hear my own voice in the silence. I learned to survive on discipline, not distraction.

I've been mislabeled many times by people who don't truly know me.

There have been many conversations where someone calls me an introvert; others mistake me for an extrovert.

It all depends on the situations they've experienced around me that reveal which side they've seen.

But the truth is, I like many people, am an ambivert.

Ambiverts are comfortable doing some pretty outlandish things that even most extroverted people would be reluctant to do. And, like introverts, they also thrive in isolation.

Sometimes, when I'm all alone, I feel most recharged.

Other times, I want to be the star of the show.

Life is complex.

People are complex.

Tribulation happens to everyone at some point.

It's not about the circumstances.

It's about grit.

It's about having the courage to sustain.

For just one more day.

In that little room, stripped of everything I thought I needed, I discovered something I never expected: a sense of self that could weather the storm. The boy who entered that room was impulsive, hungry for laughs, and terrified of being forgotten. The boy who emerged? He was quieter. Sharper. A little more broken—but also more awake. And that version of me has never left. He still shows up, in meetings and hard days and long nights. He still listens to the quiet. And he still believes that solitude—when faced head-on and respected—can build a man from the ashes.

That summer, I was sentenced to solitude—but in that sentence, I found more than punishment. I found a mirror. A forge. A teacher. I learned that silence doesn't just echo—it instructs. It forces you to see yourself, raw and unfiltered.

Chapter 7:

TUESDAY'S GONE

The year was 1993. I was eleven years old, just shy of turning twelve. Raven would've been born that year.

My brother. My maybe-best-friend. My maybe-co-survivor. But he didn't make it. Stillborn on February 9th.

I never held him. Never saw him. But I felt him. I still do.

Sometimes I wonder if things would've been different if he had lived. Would she have ever encountered depression? Would I have had someone to protect? Would we have protected each other? Would I have learned to breathe easier in that house? Would the violence have slowed—or would it have simply found a new direction? Would we have been stronger together, or would he have broken first? But those are questions for a different kind of story. This story—mine—is about surviving with ghosts and demons, and growing despite them.

I remember the day they told me. They called me into the living room like they were announcing we'd won the lottery. Big grins. My mother was practically glowing.
"Your daddy and I are having a baby. You're going to be a big brother!" she said.

It took me a second to process it. I nodded. Smiled awkwardly. Said something like, "Okay," and tried not to sound uncertain. But inside, I was spinning. At eleven, I understood what a new baby meant. It meant change. Less attention. No longer being the center of our small, strange family universe.

And at the same time… it meant hope. Something new. Something better. Maybe, just maybe, something that would bring peace.

She chose the name Raven. Said it sounded strong. Mysterious.

I didn't know anything about ravens at the time, but the name stayed with me. Later, I'd learn they were seen as omens in some cultures—messengers between worlds. Mysterious, yes. But also misunderstood. Sometimes I wonder if naming him Raven was her way of asking the universe for something powerful— something to save us. Or maybe she just liked the sound of it. But for me, the name always carried weight. Raven was the name of a hope we never got to hold.

My dad liked it too, though he didn't say much either way. He rarely did. By then, he was already fading into the background—trying to stay out of the line of fire.

My mom went into full prep mode. Baby clothes. Blankets. Bottles. She started organizing before she even began to show. She laid onesies out on the couch like they were sacred. Tiny blue socks, little mittens— folded and refolded like relics from a better life.

She even started humming again—soft melodies I didn't recognize, but they sounded sweeter than anything I'd heard from her in a long time. For a while, the house didn't feel like a war zone. It felt... expectant. Like something good might actually be coming.

But underneath all the preparation, the air in the house shifted. She was stressed. Tense. Edges frayed. Her moods began swinging faster than I could track.

One moment she'd be glowing, talking to the baby bump like it was already here. The next, she'd snap at me or my dad with a fury that made no sense.

The arguments didn't stop because she was pregnant. If anything, they got worse. Shorter fuses. Colder silences. Longer nights. And I had no one besides Adam to talk to. No one to tell.

My dad stayed quiet, drinking and smoking as usual. He spent more time out on the porch, staring into nothing, like he was practicing how to disappear. I think we all were, in our own ways.

I remember the night it happened. It was late. I was in my room pretending to sleep, listening—like always—for the tone of their voices. Always trying to read the forecast: peace or war.

Suddenly, she cried out. Not a cry of pain—not exactly. It was something else. A sound like something inside her had come undone. I jumped up and ran into the hallway. She was doubled over on the couch, clutching her stomach. My father stood there, agitated, unsure what to do.

They rushed to the hospital. I stayed behind with Uncle Renard, Aunt Joyce, and Adam, who had come over in a hurry and took me back to their place. Nobody explained anything.

That night, I stayed up late playing video games with Adam, trying to pretend things were okay. I didn't sleep. I waited. I wondered. The next morning, everything was too quiet. Uncle Renard and Adam walked with me back to the trailer.

My dad was already home, sitting at the kitchen table. A half-smoked cigarette burned between his fingers. His other hand clutched a cold cup of coffee. His face was blank.

"Is Mom okay?" I asked. He looked up at me, his eyes red, sunken. He opened his mouth, then shut it again. Finally, he said, "He didn't make it."

That was it. No tears. No embrace. No explanation. Nothing more. Just a hollow line that would echo for the rest of my life.

I stood there frozen, waiting for something else. A follow-up. A lie. Even a curse. Anything. But the silence that followed was thicker and heavier than grief. It was final. And it made me feel like I was in the way.

I never got to see Raven. They didn't let me go to the hospital. There was no funeral. No burial. Just silence. Like he'd been quietly erased—a sentence never finished. A chapter ripped out before it could be read.

A few days later, I asked if we were going to do something. A funeral. A memorial. A goodbye. My mother snapped. "There's nothing left to do," she said, like I'd asked something ridiculous. "It's over." My mother had a way of being as-a-matter-of-fact. And that was it.

She threw out the baby clothes a week later. Bagged them up and tossed them into the back of the truck like garbage.

I watched from the window, too afraid to ask why.

She slammed the tailgate shut without a word. Without a pause. With a look of disgust on her face. She never looked back. And she never seemed the same again.

She stopped taking care of herself the way she had previous done. She stopped caring about the outfits she wore. Her hair, once brushed and silky smooth from special shampoo, hung flat and oily around her temples. Even the scent of her changed—from lilac and dryer sheets to stale smoke. Her voice used to rise and fall like a song; now, it came in monotone commands or sudden shrieks.

In the weeks that followed, everything changed—but no one acknowledged it. My father became more of a ghost than a man, slipping quietly through the house like a shadow looking for a place to vanish. My mother, meanwhile, seemed to grow more intense—like the volume on her moods had been cranked up to unbearable levels. Every question I asked was met with a sigh, an eye-roll, or a scolding. She didn't want to talk about Raven. She didn't want to talk about anything, really. I was still her child, but I no longer felt like her son. I felt like an obstacle in her way.

Sometimes she'd walk past me like I wasn't even there. No hello. No touch. Not even a glance. The woman who used to call me "baby" when she tucked

115

me in had gone completely silent. I started talking to Raven in my head just to have someone to talk to.

I walked on eggshells every day, tiptoeing through silence like it was broken glass. I learned to read the house like weather—sensing mood in the slam of a cabinet or the pitch of her footsteps. My stomach would twist whenever I heard the clink of ice in a glass. I didn't call it fear back then. I just called it home.

The music played on, but it was lifeless.

That's when the drinking started to get worse. A lot worse. Her drink of choice? Wild Turkey. A bourbon whiskey known for its bite—strong enough to knock down full-grown men. But for a 5'1", 105-pound woman, it was a transformer.

And transform, she did.

The grief didn't make her smaller or softer. It made her sharper. Wilder. Meaner. Raven had become something more than just a memory to me — but to her, he became a demon. A fracture in her mind that split her open. I'd hear the clunk of the crystal glass against the cheap formica countertop—sometimes late at night, sometimes before noon. The Wild Turkey sat inside a bottom kitchen counter cabinet, under the sink like a permanent fixture. She stopped bothering with mixing it with coke and started pouring it straight up. She started staying up late into the night hours watching TV. Sitting in the dark, not really watching anything. Just sipping, smoking, staring, and occasionally muttering things I wasn't meant to hear. Other nights, I'd wake up to shouting—slurred and sharp, like she was arguing with ghosts.

It seemed that the part of her that might've loved me… dimmed. And the part of her that hated being seen, being questioned, being challenged—that part grew louder.

Looking back now, I know she broke that year—in a way she never fully came back from. Grief is a strange thing. It doesn't always look like sadness. Sometimes it looks like rage. Sometimes it sounds like screaming behind closed doors. Sometimes it smells like straight bourbon or burned food and cigarette smoke soaked into couch cushions. Sometimes it blames the people who are still alive.

I know she loved Raven. Maybe losing him tore something loose in her. Or maybe... maybe he was her last chance at control. When she lost him, she lost the story she'd written for herself—the redemption arc, the fresh start. And without that, the mask she wore slipped for good.

She never told me what really happened. I found out years later—from my grandmother—that there had been complications. That they tried but couldn't save him. That my mother refused therapy. Said she was fine. But she wasn't. She was colder. More calculating. Her pain didn't make her fragile—it made her dangerous.

In the middle of all that, I turned twelve. No birthday party. No cake. No presents. Just another day where I pretended, I wasn't hurt. Where I kept my head down and stayed quiet. Where I buried the ache somewhere no one could reach.

Somewhere in those quiet days, I started crafting a version of myself that might survive her. I became the peacekeeper. The invisible one. I stopped asking for things. I learned how to make myself small, how to turn pain into silence, how to read her before she exploded. It wasn't bravery—it was self-preservation.

I adapted quickly and became even better at internally processing emotions in a way that, on the surface, seemed stoic.

I still wonder what life might've looked like if Raven had lived—not just for me, but for her. For all of us.

Would he have softened her? Given her someone else to focus on? Would he have pulled attention away from me—enough to give me space to breathe? Or would he have just become another victim of the same storm?

I'll never know. But I do know this: His absence shaped me just as much as his presence might've. He didn't live long enough to protect me—but his memory still does and is tattooed on my right arm, Raven 2.9.93, in honor of a life he never got a chance to live.

It reminds me that I wasn't crazy. That something real was lost that year. That I had a right to feel it.

And maybe that's what it means to carry a ghost—not as a burden, but as a bond.

Chapter 8:

LAWYERS, GUNS, & MONEY

Grappling with your parents' troubles on a daily basis hardens you as a young child. It forces you to mature wise beyond your years, in more ways than one.

You start learning things most kids don't. Like how to listen without being seen. How to read a room without anyone spelling it out. You develop a sixth sense — not supernatural, just survival. You know when silence is dangerous. You recognize that a slammed door means more than frustration. You hear every whispered threat as if it's being shouted. You don't just listen with your ears — you listen with your eyes, your skin, your gut. You become a deep observer.

I'd learned to gauge danger by the sound of footsteps—heavy and deliberate meant anger brewing, too quiet meant someone was listening at doors. I knew which floor joist creaked and how to avoid them. I could tell the difference between a door closing and a door being shut with intention. Even the sound of the zippo lighter closing told a story, if you listened closely. These weren't skills any fourteen-year-old should need, but they kept me invisible when invisible meant safe.

But one night, all that careful listening couldn't have prepared me for what was coming.

It seemed like any other evening—until it wasn't.

THE DIRT ROAD

It was late afternoon, not long after dinner. The kind of quiet that pretends to be peace. The rays of the sun were starting to pop through the limbs of the oak and sweetgum trees that stood behind the trailer.

I could hear my parents in the living room jokingly having a conversation. They were watching an episode of Seinfeld. It was one of my father's favorite shows at the time. I was in my bedroom, down the hall, on the other end of the trailer going through my comic book collection searching for the perfect story to sink my mind into. I couldn't see my parents from where I was, but I knew they were sitting in their recliners. In my mind I could see the haze of smoke rising up from the char-filled ashtray that rested on a slender metal table that my dad had welded to match the height of the recliner's armrest. That was about the time I felt the tone shift.

There was a pressure in the air, something invisible but heavy. The kind of weight you feel before a summer storm rolls through — thick, unmoving, almost electric. The yelling came fast, and this time it didn't stop. The back and forth. It was a loop of bitterness and accusation, rising and falling like crashing waves. I couldn't tell you what they were arguing about. That part always fades. But the tone — that tone — never leaves you.

Then something shattered.

Not like a dropped glass. Heavier. Maybe a lamp. Maybe a picture frame. Or, it could have been the thick glass ashtray. It wasn't just broken — it was thrown. It sounded like something meant to hit, meant to harm. I still don't recall exactly what it was. But in that moment, I didn't just feel scared. I felt alone.

Not just in the room — alone in the world.

That night marked a shift. I knew it the moment I heard it in my father's voice from down the hallway. There was something in his voice I'd never heard before — something shaken. Something scared. The authority I was used to associating with his voice was replaced by a pitch that I can only describe as genuine fright.

Then the fight exploded into my room.

My father burst through the door, panicked, desperate. He wasn't yelling — he was running. And right behind him, my mother. She wasn't crying. She wasn't flailing. She wasn't bluffing. There was no hesitation — just rage, razor-sharp and deliberate. She was chasing him with a knife, and she meant every word when she said she'd kill him. Seeing him panic felt like watching Superman bleed.

What was happening? Why was he running? Why was she holding a knife?

"Robert, you need to get out of the way, son! You need to get out of the way now! This doesn't concern you." My mother said with a level of command like she was a completely different person. Like she was possessed.

It all unfolded in seconds, but those seconds stretched out like slow-motion film. I can still see it play out frame by frame. I felt the pressure inside my head begin to build, and it was as though my heartbeat was coming from within my eardrums. I relived that moment many times in the days, weeks and months that followed.

I pressed myself against the far wall and quickly backed myself into the closet. The closet, which originally had sliding panel doors was now just an opening. The doors had been removed a few years prior because they never seemed to stay on the track.

The knife was from our kitchen—the big one she used to cut pot roast on special occasions, now gleaming under the harsh overhead light in the center of the room. My father circling the small bedroom, jumping over the beds, grabbing a small object to shield himself — a chair, maybe, or one of my baseball bats. Anything to buy a second more. He darted for the hallway. The front door of the trailer was right beside my bedroom. He had passed it to come into my room.

Why?

Was he trying to draw her away from it? That didn't make sense.

Was he trying to bring me into the scene as some kind of diversion? Hoping she might stop if I was there?

Was he concerned that had it been locked it would have slowed him down?

Or was it just a panicked mistake?

Whatever the reason, after slipping past her, he bolted out the front door. The fight spilled into the yard. The yelling grew louder, more violent. It was so loud that my Uncle Renard — next door — heard the chaos and immediately called the cops. He tried to offer mediation, keeping a cautious distance between himself and my mother — his little sister. It was as if he trusted she wouldn't turn on him, but he kept space between them just to be sure.

By the time the police arrived, things had calmed. At least, on the surface.

There were two officers in the car—one older with graying temples, one younger who kept looking at me with something like pity. They didn't ask me any questions. Renard stood on the porch, his hands shoved deep in his pockets, talking in low tones to the older officer while keeping his eyes on my mother, who had suddenly become the picture of composure.

No one asked me what I saw. Not even the younger cop with pity in his eyes. Maybe I didn't look broken enough to worry about. Or maybe I looked exactly like they expected.

What I remember most clearly about that moment are a few things. The blue and red lights from the top of the police car that circled slowly as they flashed across the front of the trailer. The constant pop of light as it crossed my vision. And the sight of them handcuffing my father, placing him in the backseat and taking him away. I remember the confusion, the ache in my chest, the silent question screaming in my head:

Why him?

He was the one running! She was the one chasing him with a knife!

But in that moment, none of it made sense. Not the law. Not justice. Not even love.

It wasn't just that I saw him taken away. It was the way she stood afterward — calm, collected, even proud. Like she'd won. Like it had all gone exactly the way she planned.

Later that night, long after the police had left and the house had gone still, I sat alone in my room, trying to make sense of what had happened.

I couldn't stop thinking about that closet—how instinctively I'd crawled into it. It wasn't the first time it had felt like a place of refuge.

I used to sleepwalk as a kid. And one night, I dreamed I was trapped in the bathroom. Over and over, I stepped out of the bathtub, only to find myself back inside it. I cried until my parents found me— standing barefoot in that same closet, disoriented and confused.

Looking back now, I wonder if that dream was my mind's way of telling me something: that even when I thought I'd escaped, I was still inside the same cycle. Still stuck.

Even back then, my body was already learning how to hide.

It's a strange thing, realizing that the person meant to protect you can also be your greatest source of pain. It scrambles your compass. It teaches you to depend on yourself far earlier than anyone should have to. It causes you to become extremely guarded. Trusting someone becomes a liability.

That was when I began to understand something that would shape my life for years to come:

Sometimes the villain doesn't wear a mask. Sometimes the villain wears the face of your mother.

She would go on to rewrite the story. To me. To friends. To family. To neighbors. Especially to herself. She painted herself as the misunderstood victim, the overburdened wife, the fragile 105-pound woman who had no choice but to lash out. And I watched as the world nodded in agreement, never asking me what really happened behind the walls of that trailer.

For years I listened—her complaints, her digs at my father's family, her burdens dumped onto my shoulders. I had tried my best to console and offer advice as best as I could while only being a child. But through all of that, my love and loyalty never wavered. But that night was the beginning of me building a wall between myself and my mother.

People always say, "Your mother loves you no matter what." But what they don't talk about is when that love comes laced with fear, manipulation, or control. When love becomes a tool for guilt instead of grace.

That night didn't just change our family. It cracked open the world I thought I knew and forced me to step into a darker one. One where roles weren't clear, and nothing — not even your parents — could be trusted at face value.

I went to bed that night in silence. The trailer was quiet again, but it wasn't peace. It was the kind of quiet that settles in when the damage is done. The kind that hums like a low frequency from electricity going into an appliance you can't turn off. I stared at the ceiling for what felt like hours. The air felt heavier than it had before. Heavier than it ever would again. Not because things got better or worse. Because I became numb.

I used to think survival meant being strong. But in a house like mine, strength came second to silence.

That night taught me fear could wear a familiar face. That love, when twisted, can leave scars deeper than any belt or punch ever could. I didn't just go to bed that night — I disappeared into myself. And what woke up the next morning wasn't a boy anymore.

I've learned that silence can be louder than shouting.

That not all battles are won by fighting — some are survived by slipping between the cracks, learning to breathe quietly, and making peace with the fact that love shouldn't hurt, but sometimes it does.

It wasn't the end of my childhood. It was the beginning of my internal armor.

Chapter 9:

NOT EVEN THE TREES

The Georgia sun hung like a punishment. By midday, it baked everything — the grass, the dirt, even the air. Pushing that old mower felt like dragging a furnace behind me. Sweat rolled down my back and soaked through my shirt, stinging my eyes and leaving salt rings on the collar. My Walkman headphones clung to my head, foam damp with sweat, but I didn't care. The music was the only thing that made the hours bearable.

That afternoon, something shifted.

I had just rounded the far edge of the yard, the mower coughing over thick patches of crabgrass, when a song came through my headphones. Not Even the Trees.

"Alone, as I sit and watch the trees. Won't you tell me, if I scream, will they bend down and listen to me?"

The sound stopped me cold.

I stood there, gripping the mower handle, motionless in the middle of the yard. The blades still whirred beneath me, but inside I'd gone still. The lyrics didn't just hit — they landed like a confession I hadn't known I was making.

It felt like someone had cracked open my chest and poured my silence into song.

I didn't know it then, but I was depressed. Not just "having a rough day" sad, but something deeper. Something dull and heavy and constant. I wasn't crying. I wasn't raging. I wasn't anything. Just a dull ache behind my eyes and a constant weight in my chest. Like I was watching my own life unfold behind thick glass, unable to reach it — or care.

I was thirteen, and I thought maybe I was just broken.

Those lyrics weren't just words — they were prayer, pain, and poetry wrapped together. That first time I heard Not Even the Trees, something inside me shifted. .

At the far edge of our yard sat an old 1968 Bel Air — a classic that once gleamed in dark green paint years before I was born, now faded by time and the southern sun. Its body was speckled with rust, its tires soft with age. He had pulled the engine out of it a year earlier and swapped it over to an old Chevy C-10 to use as a work truck. The center of the metal roof was caved in just a bit from years of me jumping on top of it. My father used to talk about restoring it one day. He had gotten it from his cousin Clayton so it had sentimental value. I think he saw potential in that car — a project he could fix. Something solid. Something that made sense.

But I saw something different.

To me, that car became sacred ground. My sanctuary. Just as the porch had been for my grandfather.

After school — especially on days when home felt like a house full of sharp edges — I would make my way out there, climb on top, lay back and press play on my Sony Walkman. I'd lie back against the warm metal roof, let the sun soak into my skin, and allow the music to flood my ears and drown the chaos. It was soothing.

There were so many days I would climb up the large chrome bumper to sit on the hood and look out across the field on the other side of the dirt road. I can remember thinking about how much distance there was between me and the road on the other side of that field. I also thought about how much distance there was between me and the rest of my life. I wondered what it would be like and if better days laid ahead.

Music, that had started as a release for joy had turned into my escape — I actively sought it out. There was no Spotify back then. No YouTube. If you wanted new music, you either saved up for a trip to the store or ordered it through the mail. I remember the first time I saw the advertisement that had slipped out of the Sunday morning newspaper, and circling albums on that Columbia House catalog, lured by the promise of 12 CDs for a penny. I pored over the tiny album covers, flipping through pages like they were treasure maps. It didn't take long before I sent off for them, stuffing cash into the envelope and taping the corners so it wouldn't fall out. My parents weren't pleased because it required a commitment to purchase CDs each month. But I loved it. Weeks would go by, and I'd check the mailbox every day. When that cardboard box finally arrived, it felt like Christmas morning. Those CDs — Stone Temple Pilots, Oasis, REM — weren't just music. They were lifelines. Each one added to my little library of escape. I'd slide them into my Walkman and let the lyrics speak for the pain I hadn't yet learned to articulate.

I'd close my eyes, listening, and ask the sky questions I couldn't ask anyone else.

Why does my life have to be like this? Why did she stop smiling? Why did they argue all the time? Why did she hate my grandmother?

Sometimes I talked to God. Other times, I just talked to the silence. But I always listened back, hoping something — anything — would answer.

My mother had once been so different.

She used to take me shopping and make the day feel like an adventure. We'd go to the grocery store and she'd always let me grab a warm croissant from the bakery because she knew they were my favorite. At discount stores, she never said no when I asked for a He-Man or Ninja Turtle. She was soft. Bright. Present. Warm.

We took trips to the beach at Tybee Island, just the two of us. She'd play music with the windows down on the long drives, laughing at my made-up car games and pretending not to see me sneaking extra cookies when we picnicked on the sand.

She was happy. She seemed complete.

But something changed around the time I turned nine— before the move. That was when things began to unravel.

It was subtle at first. A shift in tone. A distance in her eyes. She stopped smiling as much. She stopped caring about the little rituals we'd shared.

And then the drinking really began.

I didn't recognize it as depression — not in her, not in me. I just knew she was gone, even though she was still in the house. And in her place was someone I didn't recognize. Someone cold. Someone quick to lash out. Someone who knew how to twist love into a leash.

I missed the mother I had known.

But when I tried to grieve her, no one else seemed to notice she was gone.

So, I climbed on top of that Bel Air. I pressed play. I closed my eyes. And I escaped.

That car knew more about my soul than anyone else did at the time. The rusted hood held my weight when the world felt too heavy. The hollow inside held forgotten magazines, cassettes and dust — but it also held secrets. My secrets. My fears. My quiet prayers. I resonated with that car. While everything around me moved uncontrollably forward, time wasn't standing still—but I was anchored. Just like the spreading rust on that Bel Air, my heart bore the same aged marks and hidden scars.

The trees surrounded that car like silent sentinels, but they never bent. They never whispered back.

Not even the trees were listening.

The chorus echoed in my ears again and again:

"I'm a stranger in my home, now that everybody's gone."

I knew what that felt like. To walk into the living room and feel like a stranger. To ask a question and receive a glare. To try and be funny and be met with silence. To battle the internal struggle of feeling like my parents were no longer the people they had been in my earliest childhood days.

That Bel Air wasn't just where I listened to music. It was where I started having real conversations with God. Desperate ones. Angry ones. Sometimes I'd shout into the sky until I was hoarse, wondering if God cared, if He was even real, if maybe I was being punished from a prior life.

But I kept talking. And I listened.

The song gave me permission to hurt.

That may sound strange, but when no one acknowledges your pain, you start to wonder if it's real. Not Even the Trees made my pain feel tangible. It named the ache. It gave me a companion in my solitude — even if that companion was just a melody carried through foam headphones.

It was the first time I ever felt my soul bleed, and I didn't try to hide it.

And it became my ritual.

I'd do my chores like cutting grass, sweat pouring down my back, and as soon as I was done, I'd park the mower back in the shed and grab a glass of sweet tea from the kitchen — cold, syrupy, and poured over clinking ice cubes. Then I'd head back outside and start shooting hoops in front of the Bel Air, the ball bouncing against the makeshift plywood backboard nailed to a four foot by four foot post my dad had built just for me.

Eventually, when my arms got tired or the sun dipped too low, I'd climb up onto the roof of the Bel Air — the spot that had molded to my shape over the years — and press play on my Walkman. The opening notes of Not Even the Trees would fill my ears, and I'd let myself fall into the sadness, one lyric at a time.

I didn't realize it at the time, but I wasn't just coping — I was surviving.

One afternoon, sitting on my bed listening to Oasis the realization hit me clearly: This feeling wasn't temporary. It wasn't just a reaction to one fight or one moment—it was a part of me now, something deep-seated and stubborn. I wasn't just a kid who was sad; I was someone wrestling with something more complicated, something that didn't vanish when laughter returned. Accepting that was very hard, but strangely comforting, because it meant my pain was valid. It meant I wasn't imagining things.

There was no therapist in my story. No counselor at school asking the right questions. No adult who pulled me aside and said, "Are you okay?"

Quit the opposite. I had been the therapist, the counselor, the confidant for my mother.

There was just the music. The metal. The trees.

And a kid trying to make sense of a world that no longer made sense.

Looking back now, I realize that Not Even the Trees was more than just a song — it was my mirror. Isolation wasn't just physical; it was emotional. I learned to be my own company, to find comfort in solitude. The loneliness forced me inward, teaching me to trust myself above anyone else. At the time, I didn't see this as strength—I saw it as a means of survival. But looking back, those lonely days spent on the Bel Air's roof shaped a core resilience in me. It taught me to find my own voice, even if the only one listening was me. It reflected my confusion, my rage, my sadness, *and* my hope. It helped me start to understand what it meant to feel deeply without knowing why.

150

It also gave me my first glimpse of my own strength.

Back then, I didn't know what healing looked like — but I knew how to endure. I didn't have answers, but I had a song. And sometimes, that was enough to get me through the quiet and the storms.

Because the truth is, I kept going. I kept showing up. I kept cutting the grass, doing my chores, keeping my head down, even when the weight of the world was unbearable.

That song didn't fix me.

But it helped me feel like I wasn't alone.

151

And that made all the difference.

"Now my days are short and my nights are long. I lay down with memories of you that keep me going on."

That's what music did for me.

It gave me memories to hold onto. It gave me space to grieve. And most of all, it gave me a voice — even when the world stood still, even when no one else was listening. Not even the trees.

Chapter 10:

THE SIGN

There's an old saying: "A true friend isn't just someone who stands beside you during the storm, but someone who walks into the darkness to find you and bring you back into the light."

The next year, I transitioned back to public school. Ninth grade. High school. By this point I had missed three years of bonding with my peers. Many changes had taken place. Some faces had moved on, while other faces were new. My cousin Adam was driving now so I was able to ride with him instead of. taking the bus, which was especially nice. I had a few familiar friends in the new environment from my years of playing rec league baseball. But many of them were either a grade above or a grade below me. And I found myself lonely traveling between classes. Always transitioning between walking with my head down but occasionally sneaking a peak around to see if I noticed someone, I knew who I could latch onto.

It was the mid-90s, and our school had started getting portable classrooms — glorified trailers, a cheap solution to overcrowding. Troubles at home had followed me like a shadow, creeping into every corner of my life. I remember thinking, Is this as good as it gets? Is this all life has to offer?

It wasn't the first day of school, but it was early in the year. I was sitting in one of those portable classrooms, bored out of my mind. The teacher droned on, and the clock ticked painfully slow. I watched the long, thin second-hand stretch time from one click to the next. Then — flick — I felt a thumb hit my right ear. Immediately, I thought of Drew. Not again.

I ignored it the first time. Then — flick — again.

At this point, I'd had enough. I spun around, ready to snap. But I stopped short when I saw a disarming grin and a friendly face. "I heard you can play pool," he said. "What?" I replied. "Yeah. I heard you're pretty good. That you play at your cousin Jesse's house." "Uhh...

yeah, I know how to play." "Well, you should come over sometime. I've got a pool table and we're always looking for another player."

His name was Richie Phillips. In that flick of a thumb, my life tilted. I didn't know it then, but I'd just met the person who would help transform everything I thought about school life.

I didn't trust it at first. Was this a setup? A joke? Some kind of prank? But Richie seemed genuine. Even though he was a lot cooler than anyone I'd ever talked to, he treated me like an equal. Like I was no different than him.

Richie was about a year older than I was and seemed to have it all — perfect hair that somehow always stayed perfect, an older girlfriend two grades above us, one of those indestructible Toyota pickup trucks, and even a 1967 Chevy Camaro. It needed some work, but it had serious potential.

Even after we started talking, I stayed cautious. But Richie wasn't deterred. He even made it a point to speak directly to my mom — told her who he was, where he lived (only seven or eight miles away), and how to get in touch by providing his home phone number. She was trepidatious, but eventually gave her blessing. Though her caution remained.

My mother wasn't the only one unsure about Richie hanging out with me. Several people in his circle also wondered why I was coming around. I was different — not for the same reasons that had plagued me at Pinewood, but because of who I'd become. I was awkward and shy by that point, no longer the outgoing, brave, bold kid who had caught the squirrel in grade school. That kid had been repressed.

At first, I went over once or twice a week. But soon, Richie and I were inseparable. We hung out nearly every day after school or after he got off work. On Friday and Saturday nights, we'd shoot pool at his place until the early hours of the morning. And some days we stayed up all night.

To me, his setup was incredible. His family was solidly middle-class, but his dad had a detached garage behind the house with three sections: a space for working on cars, a pool room, and an area for band equipment. The pool room had a roll-up garage door and a standard doorway beside it. Inside were oversized speakers and a stereo tuner — country music playing nearly 24/7. This was pre-internet, and the radio still felt magical. You'd hear a new song and have to wait for its return.

Not long after Richie and I started hanging out, I brought my cousin Adam and my friend TJ into the mix. They had felt like I disappeared the moment Richie entered the picture, but Richie was quick to ask me to invite them over.

He also had his own circle — friends everywhere — but Richie Edwards and Bubba Sloan were the two who naturally rounded out our crew. Bubba and I had played baseball together for years, and our families got along well. Somehow, our groups meshed seamlessly. But at the center of it all, it was always Richie and I. It felt like a world of possibility.

Many nights, Richie, Adam, and I rotated between shooting hoops and playing pool, living out some of the best years of our lives. Often TJ or Richie Edwards was there as well. But just as many nights Richie and I found ourselves alone, listening to the radio, shooting pool, and having conversations. We talked money. We talked girls. And we talked struggles. Richie always listened and provided honest feedback and support when I talked about the challenges I had at home. The struggles my parents would have about money, about life, and about in-laws. What we didn't know then was how fast those nights of laughter and late shots would be interrupted by something none of us were ready for.

One early morning, after a long night of shooting basketball and pool, I climbed into my truck and headed toward my grandmother's house to grab some sleep. I stopped at the Zip-In gas station on the corner, just down from Richie's, to fill up. While pumping gas, my beeper went off. Cell phones were still a luxury back then—most of us had beepers—and I recognized the number immediately. It was my Aunt Haroldian, Jesse's mom. She had punched in 911 after her number. Emergency. Aunt Haroldian was a tough woman. She was slightly rough around the edges, but still had a motherly demeanor. I dug a quarter out of my console, walked over to the payphone next to the pumps, and called her back. I wasn't ready for what she was about to say. Her voice — raspy as usual — was amped up.

"Hey boy, your mama's in the hospital," she told me. "She took a whole bottle of pills. They think she was trying to kill herself." My stomach dropped. I felt everything all at once—shock, confusion, anger, disappointment, even rage. My mind started racing, but my body just froze. It was one of those moments where the world goes quiet, like all the sound just pulls away, and you're left standing there, holding a phone, trying to make sense of something you can't believe

158

you're hearing. The thought of her laying in the living room with an empty bottle of pills ran through my mind.

I drove straight to Grandma Mary and told her what had happened before heading to the hospital. There I found my father, along with several of my mom's brothers and her only sister, my Aunt Kitty. They all wrapped their arms around me with words of encouragement and support. It was the first time I felt like someone other than my grandmother had acknowledged the depth of what had been going on and the pain I had been experiencing.

Later that night I returned to Richie's house. It had replaced the old '68 Bel Air as my sanctuary. I had called Richie earlier in the day before heading to the hospital to let him know what was going on. He had to work that evening, but told me I knew where the keys were for the pool room and that as soon as I was back home, I should head over and rack myself a game of pool. I didn't need to wait on him to get off of work.

When I got there, I didn't start shooting pool right away. I turned on the lights above the pool table, flipped on the radio and sat on the couch just staring into space. Later that evening, when Richie came home, still in his work shirt, smelling like fryer grease. He didn't ask what happened right away. He just sat next to me on the couch beside the pool table and passed me a can of Pepsi. "I've got you, man," he said. "Whatever happens next—you'll be alright. We'll ride it out." And just like that, I knew I wasn't alone.

Richie worked harder than anyone I knew. He didn't use curse words. What teenage boy doesn't curse? At least from time to time. People assumed things came easy to him, but I got to see behind the curtain and they didn't pay attention to details like I did — the tension at home, the arguments with his parents. He had a vision for how he wanted life to be, and he wasn't afraid to grind to get there. He was steady. Driven. Stubborn in all the best ways. He had will power.

I admired that about him. It started to rub off on me — at first in little ways. The way I carried myself. The way I dressed. Even how I styled my hair. Small things added up.

Back then, I'd copied my middle-part haircut from the Ace of Base video for 'I Saw the Sign.' I didn't realize how fitting that song would be. I was living a life full of signs — of pain, change, and something waiting to shift — but I hadn't yet learned to read them. I loved the song — and the haircut I copied from it. Looking back, it was one of those trends we all cringe at later. An embarrassing phase of life. Richie had urged me to change it and go a different direction.

After weeks of consideration, I finally decided to cut it. This decision didn't come easy. I was reluctant. My internal identity was tied to my external features. Having the hairstyle gave me flexibility between semi-short hair in the back with a bowl cut, to having longer hair on top. A feature that I instinctively enjoyed for the ability to go extended periods of time without a touchup.

The day I cut it off, a weight was lifted. It wasn't just a crisp new cut — it was a new identity. One I wasn't sure how to wear yet. The first lock of hair hit the floor, and that lyric played faintly in the back of my mind: 'I saw the sign, and it opened up my eyes.' For once, it wasn't just about a breakup or teenage angst— it was about seeing my life for what it was, and knowing it didn't have to stay that way.

That haircut wasn't just a style change—it was a quiet rebellion against the version of me that had formed just to survive. A symbolic break from the version of me shaped by chaos, shame, and survival. I was shedding more than just hair; I was shedding the weight of who I'd been forced to become. Like I wasn't going to let her pain define the shape of my life anymore. I didn't have the words for it back then, but I think I wanted to be seen as someone separate from the chaos — someone worth noticing.

I instantly received a lot of positive comments. Friends. Family. All of them impressed with the new look. It was like a young boy had transformed into a young man right before their eyes. It began to feel good. And while my confidence was still very lacking; inside the new external identity felt great.

He saw more in me than I saw in myself. And slowly but surely, those small changes added up. Richie never told me who to be — he just reminded me I was already someone. When I couldn't recognize my own worth, he lent me his eyes for a while. And with every laugh, every game of pool, every quiet moment when he didn't ask but just showed up—I began to believe that maybe I was more than the pain I'd carried.

162

THE SIGN

I Saw the Sign was a fun, upbeat perspective about overcoming a challenging relationship. The lyrics about life being "demanding without understanding" were accurate. Sometimes life is tough. But parts of it were also wrong. Sometimes there are people that come along that can and will "drag you up, to get into the light where you belong".

I felt better about myself. I smiled a little more. I stood a little taller. But while I'd made surface-level changes, there were deeper things — things I wouldn't even understand for years. Pain. Anger. Doubt. They didn't disappear overnight. They had to be worked out over time — with vision, determination, and a willingness to push through.

And through it all, Richie was right beside me, helping me find my voice. Unknowingly, the day we met; Richie hadn't just walked into the storm. He walked into the darkness and found me. And he stuck by my side while bringing me back into the light. One day at a time — Sweet Jesus.

He was wise beyond his years. Steady. Loyal. Kind.

And I was lucky to call him my best friend.

Sometimes, I wonder what might've happened if Richie hadn't flicked my ear that day. If I had just kept my head down, stuck in that lonely rhythm. It scares me to think about it — how different things could've turned out if no one had come looking for me. I might've stayed hidden in the shadows, believing that was all I deserved. But he didn't let that happen. Richie saw something in me. And because of that, I started to see it too

Chapter 11:

SOMETHING TO BELIEVE IN

The air had grown thick at home in those days—heavy, somber, almost like you could cut it with a knife. What was once a small home filled with love and endless potential had turned into a grim shell of itself. A relic. The drinking and cigarettes had always been there, but now they were permanent fixtures. Some days it still felt like there might be a connection, but most days, tension ruled. Conversations had become colder, more calculated. It no longer felt like a family—it felt like a house full of strangers.

Looking back now, I realize I didn't feel like a son anymore. I felt more like a roommate. My mother still vented to me, but her conversations had grown darker, heavier, and far more adult than any teenager should have to carry.

I was sixteen by then—driving, working my first job. Life outside the home had improved slightly, mostly because of my friends. That became my escape. My version of freedom.

One morning, flipping through the local newspaper, an ad jumped off the page: "Coming Soon — Wild-Gorilla Paintball"

The internet was still in its infancy, and most people didn't have a computer in their home, let alone access to the internet. Newspapers were still king of the hill.

SOMETHING TO BELIEVE IN

The ad said the new paintball field would be opening in Groveland, Georgia—roughly twenty minutes away from where I lived.

I grabbed the phone on the wall in our kitchen and immediately called Adam. He was excited, though probably not quite as much as I was. I then called Richie. He had not heard of paintball, but thought it sounded like a lot of fun. I was locked in. I saw opportunity. I loved the outdoors! Growing up in the country I had always been drawn to firearms and marksmanship. Ever since I could walk and talk, I'd been drawn to games of strategy, games like capture the flag—probably a side effect of growing up surrounded by stories of military service from and grandfathers and dad.

This brought images to my mind of my friends and I standing around a map rehearsing our gameplan, much like how it looked when my friends and I surrounded that squirrel in kindergarten so many years ago.

Images of us communicating in silence with hand signals, as we moved stealthy through the woods and across the playing field. Images of us darting behind bunkers, like real life soldiers. Only, without the grim side effects of actual military conflict.

That afternoon, I drove out to Groveland to see what I could find. I pulled up to what looked like a raw piece of land—freshly cleared, still rough around the edges—but clearly something was in the works. I stepped out of my truck and started walking around.

Then I heard a voice call out from a distance: "Hey there! Can I help you?"

I turned toward the woods and spotted a thin, scrappy-looking older guy standing just beyond the tree line. He wore a sleeveless shirt, cut off jean shorts, and boots. His arms were covered in tattoos, his hair pulled back into a ponytail, and a long goatee hung from his chin. He didn't exactly blend into rural South Georgia—he looked like he belonged somewhere else entirely.

I introduced myself, explained that I had seen the ad in the paper, and was curious about the field. His face lit up.

"Name's Lee Mitchell," he said. "My wife Donna and I just moved here to get this place up and running. We've got a lot of work to do, but it's coming along."

He started asking me questions—about school, my interests, my work. I'm not sure why, but it felt like he instantly took a liking to me. Before I left that day, he offered me a job.

I didn't hesitate. At the time, I had just recently started my first real job at Hardee's—and I hated it. Standing in one spot punching buttons all day wasn't for me. It was a physical and emotional drain. I was used to physical labor and loved being outside. Hardee's felt artificial—indoors, repetitive, and emotionally draining.

Lee told me they were in the process of renting a small shop space in downtown Pembroke. Pembroke sat between Ellabell and Groveland. As the county seat, it had a few thriving small businesses, even though it wasn't the largest city in the Bryan County.

That day, I also met Donna, their daughter Sarah, and their son-in-law Patrick.

He told me he'd worked in construction up north in Pennsylvania, but always had a dream of building something of his own. Donna had worked as a school secretary for years before they decided to start fresh down South. They hadn't come with much—just grit, some weathered tools, and a shared vision. You could see it in their eyes—they were all in, and they made me feel like I could be, too.

Donna was sweet—heavyset, quite a bit older than Lee, with a soft, motherly presence. They were an odd pair—Lee was all wiry-eyed, full of energy and grit, and Donna was calm and nurturing. But somehow, they just worked.

Before I left, they told me the job was mine if I wanted it. Just like that. Hired on the spot. Maybe it was the way I asked questions—or maybe he saw a younger version of himself. Whatever it was, he saw something in me I didn't yet see in myself.

I didn't realize it yet, but that belief—the quiet kind, the kind you don't have to earn—was exactly what I'd been missing. He didn't try to fix me. He just treated me like I was already whole.

The plan was to open the shop to sell paintball supplies and equipment, and to promote the business of the paintball field. Lee said he would need help at the field too—setting up, refereeing games, assisting customers. If I proved myself, there might be other opportunities down the line.

A few weeks went by as Lee and Patrick put the final touches on the property. I was so excited. I couldn't stand the wait. Every day I daydreamed about what might be with Wild-Gorilla.

About a month later, the first group reservation came in. It was a church group. They had heard about Wild-Gorilla in the Savannah Morning News, and thought it would be a fun experience for their youth group.

I was a bit nervous, but by then, Lee had spent a lot of time coaching me on all things paintball. We talked gear, strategy, rules—but over time, our conversations grew to include things like how to manage customers, run a safe game, and operate a business.

I don't know who was more excited about that day—the church group, or myself. The initial orientation felt like it took forever, but once we let them loose onto the field the whole world became alive. You could taste the rush of adrenaline in the air and hear the whizzing sounds as the paintballs flew past toward the enemy.

It was a blast. Everything had gone smooth that day. Just as planned. And when I walked off the field that evening I felt taller, more confident. In that moment, I felt like I was walking on air. I soaked up the energy from Lee and Patrick. They were giddy like they had just robbed a bank. I felt accomplished and for the first time in a long time, I believed in the possibilities of the future.

One of the first things that caught my attention at the paintball field was how Lee and his son-in-law Patrick played—shorts and their bright orange Wild-Gorilla referee T-shirts. I had always pictured paintball players in full camo, fatigues, even ghillie suits. I assumed it must hurt—that you needed armor, or at least camouflage. But Lee explained that sometimes, all that extra stuff just slowed you down. A minimal approach made you faster and more agile. Speed was your friend.

They treated me like family—oftentimes better than my own.

Shortly after, I started working at the paintball shop too. The field was thrilling, but the shop gave me something else—stability. Purpose. A small room that felt like my own corner of the world. I used the skills I had learned from working with my grandfather at the flea market—how to talk to people, how to sell. It all translated.

The field exploded in popularity. Every weekend, parties came out to book time slots. People drove in from over an hour away. Lee kept a logbook of where customers were coming from. But the shop itself struggled not too long after opening. The first few months it did well. But not long after that it began to decline. Pembroke was too small, too quiet. Most locals were too busy working on their farms or out hunting or fishing. They didn't buy in to the idea of running around pretending to be army men. Foot traffic just wasn't enough to keep it afloat.

Eventually, Lee broke the news. "Well, Grasshopper," he said—his nickname for me—"looks like we're gonna have to close up shop. Donna's not happy about it, and I know you ain't either. But it's just not bringing in enough to cover the bills." Then he paused and added, "You ever thought about learning how to lay pavers? It's hard work, but you're young. You can handle it."

Lee's main income came from his stonework construction business "Stone Construction"—something he'd done for decades. I told him I was interested. I needed the money. Losing the shop meant losing three- or four-days' worth of income a week. I couldn't do stonework during the week, but it paid more—so it all balanced out.

When I found out that the shop was closing, I didn't cry—but I felt something twist in my chest. That little room in Pembroke had become more than a job. It had been a second home. I used to sweep the floors like it was sacred ground. I took so much pride in building displays in the two bay windows on each side of the glass front doors. I had imagined what it would be like to own my own shop one day. Maybe a sports memorabilia shop. Or maybe a comic book store. But just like so many things in my life, that hope disappeared before it could fully bloom.

A few weeks later, a weekend opened up with no paintball bookings. I met Lee in Pembroke, and we rode together into Savannah for my first job.

That one day turned into many.

I spent hours riding shotgun in his old Chevrolet Silverado pickup truck. Working that job gave me access to so many fancy homes and neighborhoods that I had never previously been exposed to. I was in awe of just how nice those homes were compared to the ones back in Ellabell.

Lee wasn't the type to give long speeches, but his presence had a gravity to it. Like if he believed the world could make sense, then maybe it could. Riding next to him in that Silverado, I started seeing things differently. The houses weren't just rich people's homes—they were possibilities. Visions of a life I hadn't dared to dream about.

The more time we spent together, the more I saw Lee as a close friend instead of a boss. He'd give me advice on things I never heard at home. Like how to pace yourself on a job to get through the day, and incorporate efficiency into your plans before you start so that you could save time, or how to budget the little money I made. We'd stop at gas stations where he'd always buy himself a Mountain Dew and Snickers, and he would buy me a Twix candy bar and a Sprite.

"You're a good kid, Robbie," he'd say, out of nowhere. "Just keep doing what you're doing, and you'll go far."

I didn't know it then, but those words stuck with me like scripture. He wasn't perfect. He could be gruff, and I'd later learn he had his demons too. But he showed up. He paid me fair. He believed in me—and at that point in my life, that belief meant everything.

Years later, I'd catch myself offering the same advice to someone younger, realizing I was passing down the same quiet encouragement Lee once gave me.

Lee gave me more than a job—he gave me a glimpse into a life where people believed in each other. Where second chances weren't rare, they were expected. And for a kid clawing for stability, that belief was everything.

Lee's favorite band was Poison. On those long rides in to Savannah and other cities where our job sites were, he played their CDs over and over. At first, I rolled my eyes. But before long, I found myself singing along. Their songs had rhythm. They had heart.

...And they had something else.

They made you believe. Just like Poison, Lee had given me something to believe in.

Chapter 12:

CRACKED REARVIEW

The story of my mother's depression had entered a new phase. It was as if bitterness had taken root and begun to strangle everything in its path. The young, beautiful, vibrant woman she once was had become a shell of herself—cast aside and nearly unrecognizable.

Back at Wild-Gorilla, things were steady but unpredictable. Some weekends were packed with clients for paintball parties; others were completely empty. During the weekdays that summer, Lee began letting me, Richie, Adam, and a few of our other friends camp out at the property.

Those camping trips were a much-needed escape. Richie, Adam, and I, along with a few others would chip in for burgers or hot dogs, chips, and sodas. It was a break from the chaos of home—a temporary world of freedom and firelight. We'd scope out the best place to pitch our tents and gather wood for a campfire. Our chairs were mismatched—coolers, old logs, even upside-down buckets. We stayed up late, music playing in the background, swapping stories about girls, life, and the stuff we were too afraid to say during the day.

I remember one night, we roasted marshmallows on a broken rake we found by the tree line, joking that it tasted like tetanus. We laughed until our sides hurt, that kind of real, aching laughter that reminded you what it felt like to be a kid—if only for a minute.

I had also been spending more time with Lee and Patrick doing stonework. The work was hard but honest, and it kept my mind and hands busy. The contrast between having fun working at the paintball field and transitioning to the hard work of laying pavers served as a metaphor for the adolescent stage of life I was in.

Things at home, however, remained volatile. The arguments between my parents had become a daily soundtrack—predictable in frequency, unpredictable in ferocity.

But one night, things escalated.

"Get out! Pack your shit and don't come back! I don't want to see you again! Take your shit back to your highfalutin mother's house and let her cook your meals!" I heard my mother scream from down the hall.

I don't recall what my parents were arguing about. What I do remember was that my father packed some clothes and left.

The next day, I had worked a long job with Lee in South Carolina, helping on a new mall site development. It was a huge project in comparison to other job sites. Most of the time our projects were residential—someone looking to spruce up their property with either a new driveway or a backyard pool oasis. The majority of our commercial projects had been things like putting in retaining walls. The mall site was different. I knew it the moment I stepped out of the truck, as my eyes spanned across the open lot. It felt like we had miles of pavers that would need to be laid. It was a bit overwhelming and was going to keep Lee busy for weeks, if not months.

After we arrived from the long drive back that day, Donna told me that my mother had called and wanted me to call her. Something in Donna's voice sounded different. She knew the situation wasn't in a good place, but she tried her best to gloss over it, perhaps in an attempt to not upset me.

The slurred voice confirmed my worst suspicion—
my mother had been drinking.

"Robert," she said, voice uneven, "you need to
come home and get your stuff. I've had enough of
everyone and everything. I want to be left alone. In
peace."

I shook my head in frustration and started
internally talking to God. "Why does she have to be
like this? Why does she have to be so hateful?"

I just couldn't comprehend the source of her
vitriol— the sheer volume of venom she could
summon without hesitation.

As I made my way back home, I mentally rehearsed
my strategy: get in, grab a few clothes, and get out
before she could launch into another emotional

185

marathon—about how the world was crumbling around her and how my father was to blame for all of it.

But plans don't always survive contact with reality. Mine barely made it past Pembroke on the way back to Ellabell.

Sure enough, my mother had meant what she said. As I turned onto the short dirt road that led to our trailer, I saw it from a distance. There, scattered across the front yard, were all of my belongings.

My life was strewn across the lawn like leftovers from a yard sale no one showed up for. My baseball glove curled slightly from the heat. My desk drawer was half-open, papers fluttering like white flags in surrender. Even my TV—the one that I used to play Sega and Nintendo games, and watch Braves games on summer nights—sat face down in the dirt like it had been knocked out cold. My entire life, baking in the sun.

I felt my stomach drop. My first thought wasn't anger—it was exhaustion. "Wonderful," I muttered. "I've been working all day, sweating my butt off... and now I've got to haul all this back inside?" It was the last thing I felt like doing.

But when I reached the door and tried my key, it didn't fit.

"What?" I said out loud, jiggling it again. Then louder—
"What the hell?"

I knocked. Silence. No movement inside.

I wasn't just angry—I was humiliated. Somewhere deep down, I still held onto this fragile belief that I could manage things. That if I worked hard enough, kept my head down, stayed out of trouble—maybe I could keep the family from falling apart. But standing there with my key in one hand and my dignity in the other, it hit me: there was no fixing this.

"Mom?" I called out frantically. "Why is my stuff outside? Why doesn't my key work? Why are you doing this?"

After a long pause, I heard the lock click and saw the doorknob begin to turn. The door cracked open about three inches. Her face appeared in the narrow gap.

"I'm sorry, son, but you've got to go. You've got the same last name as your father and that means you're always going to be just like him. I've got to get this curse out of my life—and that includes you. You

188

can go stay with your father at his friend's house while they sit around and drink all day. And if you don't want to go stay with him, you can go to your Grandma Mary's house. Either way I don't care and I don't want to hear from you again. Leave me alone! Don't come back."

It felt like she had reached into my chest and twisted the knife that had already been lodged there for years. Her voice—those words—echoed in my mind. Flashbacks of her chasing my father with a knife began to play out like a scene in a movie I'd watched a hundred times. And just like that, the door closed and locked.

I began to pick up my things and place them into the back of my truck, heart pounding, head spinning. That day, whatever small hope I had left that things could be salvaged—burned up in that yard, alongside the rest of my life.

As I picked through my belongings, I paused on the little things. A wrinkled poster of Deion Sanders that I had hung on the wall. A cracked CD case for a Garth Brooks album. The rifles and shotguns my father gave me each Christmas. Each object felt heavier than it should have — soaked with memories, stained by silence. I stacked them carefully in the bed of the truck, trying to keep the dust off, like that would somehow preserve what they used to mean. But I knew they didn't belong here anymore. I didn't belong here anymore either.

I remembered one night, not long before things changed, when we'd eaten dinner together by candlelight from a few of their old oil lanterns, after the power had gone out. My dad grilled hamburgers outside, and my mom told stories about her childhood at the farmhouse, and how she remembered the power going out quite often. We laughed. For those few hours, everything felt normal. For a moment, we were just a family again—no yelling, no tension, just the flicker of lantern light dancing on the walls and the faint smell of charcoal hanging in the air. I remember thinking, maybe this is what peace feels like. That memory rose up now like a ghost—mocking what we'd become.

I thought long and hard about what I was going to do. My first instinct was to go straight to my grandmother's—I didn't even have the phone number to the friend's house where my father was staying. Once I finished loading up, I got inside my truck, cranked it up, and began to drive away.

As I reached the end of the dirt road, I glanced into my rearview mirror. The trailer—the place that had been my home, my battleground, my prison—shrunk smaller and smaller with each bump in the road. My life, once tethered to that broken place, was now packed into the bed of my truck. In that cracked rearview mirror, I didn't just see a home fading in the distance. I saw the last thread of boyhood unraveling. And as the road ahead unspooled before me, I realized: the past wasn't behind me—it was packed up in the bed of that truck, too. And I'd carry it for a long, long time. I fought back the urge to cry because in that moment, I felt defeated. And maybe those cracks in the mirror weren't distortions after all — maybe they were the only reason I could finally see things for what they were.

When I arrived at my grandmother's, I let her know what was going on and can recall the level of disappointment on her face, and the sound in her voice. She didn't say anything at first. Just pulled me into her arms and held me longer than usual, the soft cotton of her blouse pressed against my cheek. Her house smelled like Ivory soap and homemade beef stew — a scent that somehow reminded me I was still loved.

"Son," she said, her voice low and steady, "your mama's not right in the head. She's sick in ways the world doesn't always understand. And I'm sorry— Lord knows, I'm sorry—for what she's put on you through."

She pulled back just enough to look me in the eyes. "But hear me now and believe me later: this is not your fault. You didn't break her, and you can't fix her. What you can do is keep moving forward. Focus on yourself. Focus on building a life that's better. That's yours."

She told me I was welcome to stay with her as long as I wanted. I thanked her and unloaded my belongings into one of the spare bedrooms. Then I told her that I would be back later, that I wanted to go see my dad and talk to him about what was going on.

My father had taken refuge in a spare bedroom at a friend's place. Compared to our trailer, it felt like a castle. Satellite TV. A tidy kitchen. A giant satellite dish out front that seemed almost futuristic. I didn't know what impressed me more—the sheer size of the dish or the endless number of channels it pulled in. It was a bachelor pad with creature comforts I was not used to. There was a NASCAR race playing on a large screen TV. I wasn't into the sport, but remember thinking about the satellite dish and what all the other channel options must have in store. Across from the massive large-screen TV was what seemed like a large brand-new couch and recliner. I stood in the kitchen, staring at a clean counter and a loaf of fresh bread. It was nothing fancy, but the calm was deafening. No yelling. No tension hanging in the air like smoke. Just the hum of the refrigerator and the soft glow of the big screen television in the background. I didn't realize how starved I was for stillness.

Part of me wanted to stay there. To let this be a new chapter.

But even then, I knew: home isn't just a roof or four walls. It isn't fancy things. It's where you're wanted. Where you're safe. And sometimes, that place has to be built from the ground up. And most importantly, from within. That was the moment I stopped searching for home in other people—and started trying to build it for myself.

I used to think looking back helped you understand where you came from. But sometimes, that rearview mirror cracks. Truth distorts. Memories blur...

And if you're not careful, you start believing the broken version of the past is the whole story. That day, standing on scorched grass surrounded by the wreckage of my childhood, I realized: I had to start looking forward—even if the road ahead was just as broken and far less traveled.

Chapter 13:

MYSTIFY

Infidelity is one of the number one reasons for divorce. It hurts many people within its path. Often, young children of parents impacted by divorce due to infidelity are sheltered in some type of way. And other times they're not.

I certainly can't say that I ever expected this chapter of life to fold out the way it did—not at that point. I knew my parents had a lot of issues. They fought like cats and dogs all the time. But that had become my normal, and so I just thought that's the way life was meant to be. Losing Raven had taken a major toll on my mother's mental state, and it seemed like every day her drinking was getting worse. She finally began taking medication for her depression. And, I was starting to grow accustomed to her being belligerent, and the memory of the mother I once had was slipping away—faster than I realized.

My mother had become filled with hatred. She abandoned the small joys that once lit up her world—gardening, old movies, the laughter of friends, even music. And the negative conversations about my grandparents began to morph into conversations about other relatives including one's from her side of the family. She started speaking very negatively of my Aunt Joyce—Adam's mother. But most notably, and most painfully, were the conversations about my father.

It was extremely difficult then to hear the things she said, and it's still difficult now to write them down. But it wasn't just the words. It was the look on her face—like there was this slow-burning anger trapped within her small frame, churning and compressed so tightly it was ready to explode at any moment. My best description would be that the demon within her mind

198

from the loss of Raven and the demon in the bottle of Wild Turkey had fused together in a volatile fashion, creating someone I didn't recognize. Someone I was fearful of.

"Your father is a no-good piece of shit. And that's because he comes from your Granny and your Grandma Hendry, and they're pieces of shit!"

Granny was my grandmother Marys' mother—my great-grandmother. She lived with my grandparents during my early childhood years until she passed away in the late '80s. I remembered her warm hands and gentle humming, sitting in her recliner with a crocheted blanket over her knees. Now her name was being weaponized, pulled into something it didn't deserve.

"They think I'm white trash. Well, I might be white trash, but I'm your mother and I know I raised you right. They can kiss my ass. I'll snatch that wig off your grandmothers' head in a heartbeat and beat the shit out of her."

I was too young to know how to carry words like that. I didn't even know what to say back. I just stood with my head sunken toward my shoulders in an act of mercy. Hoping it would send the message that I was scared—helpless. Unsure what to say or do.

Writing them now makes my chest ache and my throat tighten. But it also brings on a feeling of deep sadness—not just for myself, but for her. For all the people who have walked that same path of becoming unrecognizable to their own children. Did she understand the magnitude of the transformation she went through? Could she have controlled it? Helped prevent it? She was only seventeen when I was born. Was the stress of raising a child as a child part of the problem?

Naturally, I wonder if I could've done anything differently, even though I was just a child. Could I have been quieter? More obedient? Could I have hugged her more? Listened harder? Prayed louder? Mustered up better responses or advice when she vented?

Truthfully, the answer is no. But it still hurts to think about how kind and gentle my mother once was, and how many people throughout history—and all over the world—have either lived through the pain of watching a loved one change... or been the one going through the changing themselves.

Eventually, my mother came to the conclusion that part of her problem was that she had too much time on her hands. She thought that going back to work might help her mental state. So, she went and found a job to get active and stay busy.

Throughout my childhood, she bounced between different jobs: working in the meat department at the local grocery store, cleaning hotel rooms as a maid, and for a good stretch of time, she was simply at home—alone with her thoughts, her bottle, and her grief.

Sometimes, when she was working as a maid, she'd take me along with her. She'd unlock one of the empty rooms and let me hang out while she cleaned. I'd lay across the neatly made bed, flipping channels for hours. On one occasion, Nothing but Trouble was playing on HBO—Dan Aykroyd, Chevy Chase, John Candy, and Demi Moore. We didn't have HBO at home, so it felt like a luxury. I laughed again and again at the zaniness of that movie, lost in the absurdity and chaos on screen, even while a different kind of chaos swirled just outside that door. For those few hours, things felt normal. Safe. Like the world had paused just long enough for me to laugh.

She had always dreamed of something more, though. She used to talk about going to school to become a paralegal. Her eyes would light up when she imagined herself in that role—organized, respected, maybe even with a small office of her own.

One particular evening not too long after starting her new job, she came home with a surprise. A small dog. She smiled, her cheeks red from the cold or maybe the bottle—hard to say. She held the dog in her arms like a baby and introduced her as "Macy." Macy had long wiry hair, yappy energy, and a habit of trembling even when nothing was happening. I wasn't a fan. I liked big dogs—real dogs. The kind you could throw a ball to, run with, wrestle. Like Chip had been. Macy wasn't that.

But my dad? He took to Macy right away. He chuckled at how she followed him around the house and let her jump up on the couch next to him. He even called her "the princess". I rolled my eyes, but even I had to admit—Macy had brought a flicker of something different into the house. A pause. A breath. A moment of light in a place that had been so heavy for so long.

Sometimes, when the world feels off-kilter, we latch onto small things to make it feel normal. A meal. A routine. A pet. Macy became that for my dad—a sliver of comfort in a house losing its center. I didn't know it yet, but even comfort can lie.

What I didn't know then was that it was only the calm before the storm.

One night, a few months later, I was in my room playing video games. I was playing Streets of Rage — one of my favorite Sega games. The chaos on screen was fun, absurd, cartoonish. It felt safe. Predictable. I liked games like that. No matter how loud or messy things got, there were always rules. You knew who the enemies were. You had health bars, checkpoints. Real life didn't have any of that. I remember thinking for a second, maybe tonight will be quiet. Maybe everything's finally cooling down.

My mom was at work, so it was just me, my dad, and Macy. The hum of the TV and the clicking of the controller had become a comfort, a small escape. That was before I realized the freight train that was about to hit me, head on.

I heard my dad's footsteps in the hallway. Slow. Heavy. He knocked lightly, then opened the door and walked in. His face was pale, almost gray. His eyes had a glassiness I hadn't seen since his own father died. Something was off.

He said, "Robbie, I have to tell you something. Your mother is seeing another man. She's cheating on me." Before he broke down and began to cry.

My heart dropped into my stomach. I felt like I couldn't breathe. He raised his hand and held out a crumpled piece of paper—a letter. It looked ordinary, but it might as well have been a grenade.

My fingers tingled as he held it out. I didn't want to take it, didn't want to touch it. As if doing so would make it real. I just stared at the paper, its edges worn from being handled, like it had been read over and over again.

My brain was trying to do two things at once— believe him and protect her. A part of me still wanted to think there had to be a mistake. That this was all a misunderstanding. That she wouldn't... she couldn't.

But the look in his eyes? That told me everything I needed to know. He wasn't just hurt—he was broken.

"She left this in the dresser. I found it today."

I don't remember much of what was said after that. The shock was too overwhelming. Even with all the terrible things my mother had done or said over the years, in my heart she still held a sacred space—she was still my mom. The woman who once let me pick out He-Man toys at the store. The one who used to sing along to the radio and buy me croissants on grocery trips.

And just like that, with one confession, that sacred image was shattered.

I dreaded her coming home that night. I knew things were about to explode. The tension in the house felt like static in the air, thick and dangerous. I didn't know what my dad would do. I wasn't even sure what I would do. The feeling of disappointment smothered me like a weighted blanket. I didn't know for certain what my father felt inside, but I knew I felt betrayal.

When she finally came home, the war began.

Shouting. Slamming. Glass breaking. I stood in the hallway, frozen. My heart was pounding so hard it hurt. I couldn't look away, but I didn't want to see either.

She admitted it. Said his name—Lonnie. Said she met him at work. Said he treated her better. Said he made her feel seen. That my father didn't love her the way he should. That his mother—my grandmother— had tormented her. All the blame came rushing out like a flood.

And then, after what felt like hours of arguing, my father packed a bag. Just a few clothes. A toothbrush. His shaving kit. He stood at the door for a second, looked at me, and then walked out into the night.

As if all that wasn't enough, during the arguing my mother dropped one more bomb.

Macy was from Lonnie. He had given her to my mother.

It was a dagger. I no longer just disliked the dog—I hated it. Macy represented a lie. A planted gift. A thread that had been sewn through the seams of our lives without us even knowing. My dad had loved that dog. Cared for her. And now I realized—she was part of the betrayal. I looked at her curled on the couch—eyes blinking, tail twitching—and for the first time, I saw not a pet, but a symbol. She wasn't just a dog anymore. She was proof that betrayal could be wrapped in affection. That something that made you smile could also be the thing that gutted you.

My mother hadn't just lied—she had crafted a version of our life that wasn't real. And worse, she let us live in it.

I used to think she was fragile—damaged but still good. But that night, the glass I'd placed her behind finally cracked.

She wasn't the woman who took me shopping or let me pick out action figures anymore. She was someone I didn't know. And maybe never really did.

That night, the house was quiet in a way that didn't feel peaceful. It felt hollow. Like someone had carved out the center of our lives and left us with just the shell. INXS album Mystify played, one of her favorites, as she drank away her sorrows. It set an ominous tone. The lyrics blurred into the background, but the tone was almost mocking. A song about being enchanted by someone. I didn't feel enchanted. I felt erased. The house didn't feel like a house anymore. It was like the walls had absorbed every echo from their fight. The kitchen still smelled like old bacon grease and Pine-Sol. My dad's shoes sat next to the hallway in the living room like they were waiting for him to come back. Macy curled up on the couch as if nothing had happened, her small eyes blinking without guilt. Every creak of the floorboards that night felt louder than it should've been. I couldn't sleep.

I lay in bed crying and stared at the ceiling, replaying the scene again and again. Every word. Every shout. Every tear. I didn't know what would happen next, but I knew things would never go back to the way they were. At that age, I didn't fully understand what cheating meant — not like adults do. But I knew enough. It meant someone had broken a promise. That the person who was supposed to love you most had chosen someone else. It made everything unstable. Was love just temporary? Was family just a house of cards? I had no words for it then, but the foundation I thought I was standing on had cracked — and I didn't believe it could be fixed.

And in some strange way, that was the most painful part.

Chapter 14:

INTO THE MYSTIC

About four years had passed by, living at my grandmothers, and the time had come that I was ready to move out into the world. At 20 years old Adam and I made the decision to finally make that old dream come true, and share an apartment together. He had just secured a job with the Army Corps of Engineers after graduating from Georgia Tech, and I had taken my first salaried leadership role at Walmart.

I maintained an open, but distant relationship with my parents. They didn't stay separated very long after the affair, and had worked things out as best they could. My mother would call me regularly to check on me and to vent about life, no different than before.

Occasionally I would stop by to visit them. But as I grew older and took on more responsibility, I found the stress from those phone conversations wearing on me more and more. I began to realize that I had a choice—to continue to accept it, or choose a different path.

This time period was difficult—not because things had necessarily gotten worse, but because my mother's drinking had not gotten any better. At this point, our phone conversations were either depressingly negative or erratic, drunken episodes filled with venom and hate about family and life.

In late 2004, I finally found the courage and made the decision to move on with my life. I started ignoring my mother's calls altogether, and the voicemails were growing more and more pointed. A job transfer was in the works that would take me to a new city in Central Georgia—an opportunity to start fresh. So, I changed my phone number, only shared it with my closest friends and cut all ties with my entire family, except for Adam. That decision brought me a true sense of peace.

I had found myself wondering: "How would it feel if I just walked away?" "What's stopping me?"

It was unconventional. I didn't know anyone who had simply walked away from their family altogether— it was a road less traveled, a step into the unknown. But once I made the decision, I moved on quickly. And to my surprise, I never felt the urge to look back. It felt like an enormous weight had been lifted off of my shoulders.

And that was the end of that chapter. I stepped away from my past, started fresh in a new city, and for over fifteen years, I didn't look back. Years passed in silence. I changed job roles. I changed cities. I built a life, fell in love, became a father. I never dialed their number. I never looked back.

But time has a way of softening hard edges—or at least making you wonder if the sharpness was ever justified. And in 2020, the world changed.

And so did something in me.

By then, I had advanced deep into my career and built a family of my own. I was on a path I could be proud of.

But as the world changed with the pandemic, I found myself feeling a twinge of guilt.

"Was I robbing my children of childhood joys by not having grandparents in their lives?" I thought to myself.

It wasn't just about them missing out on birthday gifts or holiday visits. It was about legacy. About roots. About whether I was doing the right thing by building a clean slate—or if, in doing so, I was erasing a part of where I came from.

I wondered: Would my daughters grow up one day and ask why they never met their grandparents? Would they see me as the villain in a story I had worked so hard to survive?

I was afraid—afraid of what I might reignite. That fear collided with hope. Maybe… just maybe… they had changed. Maybe time had softened them. Maybe they were ready to meet me as I was now—not as the scared boy I used to be, but as a man, a husband, a father. Maybe the people who had once hurt me might now be able to love my children better than they loved me. That they had changed. Or that I had changed enough to handle it if they hadn't.

It was a difficult situation. I spent many hours over the following weeks contemplating what to do. I prayed for clarity—for God to give me peace. I leaned on my wife, Leah. She had been my rock for the past ten years at that point, and I trusted her insight and judgment—though I knew she couldn't fully understand the depth and gravity of the childhood scars I would be opening. She hadn't lived through those years of trauma and pain.

There was so much turmoil deeply rooted in my relationship with my parents—wounds she didn't yet know. I had shared occasional stories about the trials I faced growing up, but never the full extent.

Finally, I decided that the right thing to do was to reach out, extend an olive branch, and make a good faith effort to move on from the past. I couldn't control the outcome, and I knew I might regret the decision, but I also knew that's how life works. I remembered the doubt I had before choosing to leave

218

all those years ago. In my mind there was a voice saying "You either take a chance and live with the results of your decisions, or you sit on the sidelines and dwell on what might have been."

So, I picked up the phone and reached out to Adam. I asked him if he could get my parents' phone number. I know it caught him off guard, but he happily obliged.

The day finally came when I made the call. I'd be lying if I said I didn't feel a wave of doubt and trepidation rush over me as I pressed the final digit and hit send. The phone rang a few times before being picked up by my Uncle Don.

"Hello?" Don said in a slow southern drawl.

"Is this Uncle Don?" I asked, recognizing his voice.

"Uh, yeah." He responded.

"Hey, this is Robbie. Are my parents around?" I asked before being cut off.

"Robbie? Robbie Hendry?" He responded in a nervously excited tone. "Yeah, hang on one minute. I'll go get her."

I could hear his excitement as he called for her in the background.

Then came my mother's voice—extremely cautious, as if she expected some kind of bad news. But after a few minutes of talking and me explaining the purpose of my call, her tone began to soften. I told her I wanted to introduce her and my father to their grandchildren. Her voice shifted from caution to a sense of glee.

Before we ended the call, we scheduled a day for them to come down to Florida for a weekend visit. My children were five and three at the time and didn't fully understand what was happening. Deep down, I felt terrible. They were young, but how could I explain their grandparents' absence from their lives up until this point? They seemed excited about meeting new people who would love them, care for them, and most importantly—buy them gifts on their birthdays and Christmas.

When the day finally came and the doorbell rang, I opened it to find the two people I had spent so many years avoiding. I was staring at my pain face-to-face. The sad, distant gaze in my mother's eyes was still there, just as I remembered. My father, on the other hand, had changed dramatically. They explained he had recently retired and was doing well, but he wasn't the same man I remembered. He had lost a lot of weight and was down to about 135lbs. His hair had turned completely gray, grown long in the back, and his face, sunken, was framed by a long, wiry beard. Still, he grinned from ear to ear and gave me a big hug. My mother, in her consistently awkward way, just stood there, unsure of what to do. I invited them in and introduced them to my family.

My mother was taken aback with the entire event. She was extremely excited about meeting her two granddaughters, but she didn't know how to process everything else. She had lived a sheltered life and had never been out of the State of Georgia. She had grown up in the old farm house built in 1845 and then the trailer that was built in 1979. Our house, the property and our cars were nice for today's standards, but to her it was unbelievable. She referred to our house as "the mansion" and acted as if she was in a foreign land.

Things that first trip seemed somewhat normal. Sure, my mother was still awkward and came across as someone unhappy with life, but it felt like she was really trying—putting on her best face. She knew the stakes were high. It wasn't just our relationship on the line anymore; multiple lives could now be affected.

Unfortunately, a tiger can't hide its stripes. Eventually, the past will always come to light.

Just a few weeks into reconnecting, I got a phone call one evening. It was my mother. She wanted to let me know how she felt about my wife, Leah. She accused Leah of neglecting our children because she was on her cell phone too much. She said I was too focused on work, money, and too obsessed with maintaining an extravagant lifestyle.

We had moved into our dream home earlier that year, and I had been fortunate enough to be able to put a large down payment on it from bonuses I had saved while being a Store Manager.

It was close to three thousand square feet and built on a stem wall foundation, which raised it several feet off the ground, unlike most homes that are built on slab foundations nowadays. It had a huge front porch like my grandparent's old farmhouse, but this one had a paver floor. It also had a large screened-in back porch that was larger than any other house we had owned, but was a bit smaller than the front porch. Both the front and back side of the home had second story balconies that gave amazing views of the natural preserve in the back and the surrounding homes in the front. It sat on a pie shaped lot, so the backyard was massive and private with large oak trees on each side. It was impressive, and certainly more than I ever thought I would be able to own.

But I had been smart with my money, savvy in my research, and been lucky enough to be in the right place at the right time when we found it. And we had been fortunate enough to have paid off both of our vehicles. They were nice, but they weren't brand new.

I felt heat rise in my chest. My fists clenched instinctively, even though I wasn't angry—I was hurt.

Leah had supported this entire effort. She had opened her heart willingly to two strangers for my sake—for our daughters' sake. And now she was being judged by someone who didn't know the first thing about her.

I took a deep breath and paused. I could feel the old me—the child version—wanting to shrink. But I wasn't that boy anymore. I had built a life. I had a voice. And I wasn't going to let her shatter what I had built.

I felt my stomach tighten. I wanted to yell, to defend my wife like she deserved. But I knew how that story ended. And I wasn't going to give her that power again. So I took another breath. I grounded myself in the life I had built—the peace, the joy, the family I protected.

"This isn't how you start over," I told her, calm but firm.

I reminded her that Leah had supported the decision to reconnect and had done so with an open heart. My mother needed to be more appreciative, not critical.

Then, just a few days later, another call came. This time, my mother sounded intoxicated. She accused my father of cheating on her, saying she had found medication in the bathroom cabinet that she believed was for sexual performance. My father had explained it was prescribed for a heart-related blood flow condition, but she refused to believe him. Her mind raced with baseless accusations.

I could hear my father arguing with her in the background, telling her to leave me out of it and stop bothering me. He understood what her actions could cause. I agreed. I told her that I didn't appreciate being pulled into their problems. I reminded her that this was exactly why I had walked away years ago. The constant drama. I was tired of being her unsolicited therapist. I told her it wasn't fair for me, as a child, to have been forced to carry the emotional weight of adult problems all those years.

She began crying. She told me she was sorry—that she understood, and that I was right.

The next time they visited, she pulled me aside shortly after they arrived. She asked if I would keep something in one of my safes and pulled out a medium sized paper sack. It was about ten inches in height and the bag had wrinkles that showed its age. She said it was more secure than hiding it under a mattress or in a closet like she had been doing for years. I agreed, and didn't think much of it.

And just when I thought things had settled—when I thought maybe we were building something new—the phone rang again. And with it came the reminder: the past doesn't stay buried just because we stop digging.

Chapter 15:

KEEP ME IN YOUR HEART FOR A WHILE

The morning of Tuesday, August 17, began like any other. I got up and went through my typical morning routine before getting ready and heading out for my day. I was at work when my phone rang. It was around 9:30 AM. I was busy, but pulled my phone out to check the caller ID. It was my dad's cell number, so I sent it to voicemail, as I often did while working. The message that followed, though, was different.

It was my mother.

Most of our recent conversations had been strained. Cordial at best. I wasn't eager to pick up when I saw my dad's number pop up because I knew it was most likely her calling. When the voicemail notification popped up, I didn't think much of it—she always left a message, even for small talk. About forty-five minutes later I got around to listening to it. But this one was different.

"Hey Robbie, it's Mama," she said in a somber tone. "I was hoping you'd pick up, but I figured you were busy. I just wanted to let you know that I'm sorry for how awful I've treated you all these years. I want you to know that I truly couldn't help it. This will be the last time you'll hear from me. I have to go away. You've got two beautiful daughters that are sweet and innocent, and I don't want to corrupt them and cause them pain the same way that I've caused you pain. I hope you'll find it in your heart to forgive me," she said, her voice cracking under the weight of held-back tears. "I love you. Goodbye."

KEEP ME IN YOUR HEART FOR A WHILE

I sat there, phone still in my hand, staring at the wall. Part of me wanted to call her right back. Another part didn't want to open that door. She had cried wolf before—dozens of times. But something in her voice was different this time. Defeated. Final. Ominous.

I played the message again. And again. Trying to hear something between the words. Some signal I had missed. I thought to myself that she must be leaving my father for a while to disappear. She was always cloaked in drama. My stomach turned, but I still told myself: "She's just trying to get attention again. She always does this." Then I felt ashamed for thinking that. Because what if this was the one time it was real?

About two hours later, my phone rang again. Same number. This time, I was on lunch and picked up—frustrated, expecting to have one of our typical conversations.

"Hello!" I said. Feeling my blood pressure start to raise.

But it wasn't her.

And it wasn't my dad.

It was a soft voice on the other end of the line.

"Um, hello. Is this Dennis' son, Robbie?" the voice asked, before quietly explaining that he was a doctor.

He asked if I could step to somewhere private and sit down to have a conversation. My heart sank immediately. My mind began to race. Was she gone? Was he gone? Did she hurt someone else? Were they both gone? I feared the worst.

The doctor—young, maybe my age, but possibly younger—told me gently that my mother had shot herself. He sounded unsure, like he was still learning how to deliver this kind of news. He said she shot herself in a way that she was not going to survive. And that my father was there at the hospital but that he was too upset to speak.

I felt a wave sweep down from my temples to my lower chest. Almost like a sigh or calmness. Not relief, just calmness.

I think I surprised him with how calm I was. Steady. Numb. I asked questions. He told me my father was okay, but was in shock and couldn't speak clear enough to hold a conversation. I thanked him and asked him to let my father know I was on the way, ended the call, cleared my schedule for the week, packed a bag, and drove to Georgia.

When I got to the hospital, my father sat in the emergency ICU room, shirt stained with blood from holding her. He looked like a man struck by lightning and somehow survived—but just barely. Just like the night he had found the letter, he was broken. But this time was far worse.

He clutched her purse like an anchor, unaware. Like letting go would make it all final. His eyes weren't just red—they were vacant, like the world had stopped making   sense.

I sat next to him, and for a few minutes after I calmed him down, we said nothing. Just breathed in the sterile air. Just existed. Sometimes silence is the only language grief understands.

Eventually, he broke it. "She said she was sorry this morning, right as I was getting into the shower." he whispered. "She told me she was sorry, and I didn't know it meant goodbye. I thought everything was

234

normal. It's my fault. I missed it." As he started to cry again.

He said the police had detained him for nearly an hour, questioning him like a suspect. Objectively, I understood. But for him, it was torment. Answering questions while in shock. Reliving the moment. Waiting, helpless. Not knowing if she was going to live or die.

My mother had been transferred from Statesboro, where the incident took place, to a trauma unit in Savannah by helicopter and kept alive by machines. The doctors gave her less than a 5% chance to live— and if she did, she'd be in a vegetative state. Her brain had suffered too much damage. She laid there, technically still alive, but no brain activity.

I booked a hotel room nearby and convinced my dad that he needed to sleep and that there was nothing anyone could do outside of what the doctors were doing. Sleeping in the chair wouldn't help. And neither would staying. At least a few hours in a bed might offer a moment to breathe.

That night I laid in the bed staring up at the ceiling, much like I had in my youth when things had exploded at home. I thought about the words that the doctor had said. "She's technically still alive, but there's no light on. No brain activity. I wondered if that meant her soul was no longer with her body or somewhere else. It all felt surreal.

My father broke down again on the second day. We began the painful process of preparing for the next steps. Lots of paperwork at the hospital and planning the funeral.

Anger. Resentment. Relief. Those were the emotions I felt during those days. Relief that the chaos might finally be over. That the pain, the drama, the drinking, and the violence might finally come to a close and be put to rest.

But beneath that, there was still a little boy clinging to the mother he remembered.

Family came. Adam was there on day one. My father offered to let me visit the room with him, but I declined. I wasn't ready. I didn't want to see her that way. When my uncles, two of her three older brothers arrived—Buddy and Daus—it hit me hard. Daus looked exactly like my grandfather. When I saw him as I stepped off the elevator, I finally crumbled. It was like seeing a ghost. It was the only time I cried during the entire time, including the funeral.

When it came time to coordinate the funeral my father seemed to do a lot better than I had expected. He requested several of her favorite songs to play on repeat in the background and the thought resonated and stuck with me.

The funeral was small, but more attended than I expected. Friends. Family. Several of my childhood friends. But no one from my father's side. That part hurt. I had hoped his brothers would show up for him. Put the past aside to support their flesh and blood. But after years of division between my mother and them, I guess I shouldn't have been surprised.

That day was tough. I really didn't want to be there. But I wanted to support my father. I kept my distance from the casket the entire time and I wasn't exactly sure why. I just knew that I didn't want to see her. I didn't feel the need to say goodbye.

I've thought about that distance ever since. It wasn't that I didn't care. It was that part of me had already been grieving for years. Decades, even. Mourning the mother I'd lost, long before her physical death. The woman who once held my hand in the grocery store. Who once fried pork chops for dinner with black-eyed peas and rice. Who once danced

238

barefoot in the kitchen while cleaning. That loved to lay out in the sun and tan. That version of her had died long—long ago.

The woman in the casket was a stranger shaped like someone I once loved. And maybe standing far away was my way of honoring what was real—what once was.

Or maybe I was afraid that if I got too close, the grief would finally catch up—and bury me with her.

After the funeral, life moved forward. Slowly. Quietly. But something inside me had shifted. I didn't just want to move on—I wanted to heal.

Months later, I was out on a trip with friends when "Free Bird" came on the speakers overhead. One of my mother's favorites. She and my dad had seen Lynyrd Skynyrd live years ago back in the late 70's. She once gave me a poster from that concert.

"If I leave here tomorrow, would you still remember me?" rang out and hit me like a gut punch.

I excused myself to the bathroom as my eyes filled with tears. The song felt like her voice again, reaching through time, through pain, through memory.

I didn't fight it. I let the tears come. Embraced the moment.

And in that moment, I realized something: I was okay.

As difficult as some of those times had been—life goes on. And just like that rusted '68 Bel Air, everything has a time and a place before time marches on.

It was okay that she was gone. It was okay to grieve. It was okay to move on.

Time passed. Life moved on. But something in me refused to stay silent anymore.

For years, I struggled to talk about my childhood — about my parents, the drugs, the abuse, the neglect, and the constant instability. I wondered if I'd end up like my mother or her brother — trapped in the same cycles of mental illness. I knew I suffered from anxiety and perfectionism, always chasing approval I was never sure I deserved.

But healing came from an unexpected place. One day, while listening to an interview with a trauma expert, I heard him mention something called CBT — Cognitive Behavioral Therapy. It piqued my curiosity, so I picked up a copy of 'When Panic Attacks' by Dr. David Burns, one of the pioneers of cognitive therapy.

That book fit like a glove. It gave me language for my pain. Structure for my thoughts. Permission to begin again.

For years, I struggled with dizziness and chest pains whenever I felt like I was under the microscope at work. I always chased perfectionism because I never felt like I was good enough. I had developed many of my own methods to cope. And it had been very successful. But CBT taught me how to understand, respect and process those feelings as just that— feelings. Nothing more.

I can't change the past. I carry regrets, just like anyone does. But I also carry strength. Resilience. A deeper sense of purpose I wouldn't trade for anything.

KEEP ME IN YOUR HEART FOR A WHILE

If you've read this far, my hope is that you feel seen — that something in these pages reminded you of your own courage. That maybe, you found a little more understanding for yourself, or for someone you love.

If you've ever felt trapped by your past—like love came with strings or shame—you're not alone. I've been there. And I promise: there's a way out.

Trauma does not define you.

Your story doesn't end with what happened to you — it begins with how you respond. You already carry within you everything you need to heal: insight, grit, grace.

Sometimes, all it takes is stepping back... observing, listening... and following the subtle cues — the breadcrumbs God places in your path to guide you home.

243

May you write your own melody, built from both pain and perseverance. And may it become your greatest hit that provides you comfort along the path.

And when the road feels long or uncertain, remember — even dust-covered dreams can bloom again when met with light. You are not broken; you are growing.

God bless you. God bless your friends and family. God bless everyone who's dealt with trauma. And God bless America!

Epilogue:

LIFE IS A HIGHWAY

If you've made it this far, thank you. Writing this book wasn't easy. Living it was even harder. But I'm still standing. And that, in itself, is a miracle.

I didn't write The Dirt Road just to rehash the pain—I wrote it to name it, so it would no longer own me. There's power in naming your story. In laying it out, dirt and all, and saying, "This happened—but it doesn't define me."

Growing up the way I did, there were days I didn't think I'd make it. I carried shame like a second skin. I feared I'd turn out just like the people who hurt me. And for a long time, I kept quiet—because silence was safer than vulnerability.

But somewhere along the road, I found my voice. Sometimes in solitude. Sometimes in therapy. Sometimes in late-night conversations with God, my wife, or a lifelong friend.

If you saw yourself in these pages, I hope you found more than pain—I hope you found echoes of strength. The kind of strength that comes not from having it easy, but from refusing to quit. From learning to build peace with your past without letting it dictate your future.

I know what it means to be the kid who didn't feel safe in his own home. I know what it's like to sit quietly in a classroom while carrying more than any child should have to bear. I know the ache of watching someone you love become someone you don't recognize.

But I also know what it means to grow beyond it.

To find healing through therapy, faith, friendships, fatherhood, and love. To discover joy in the smallest of moments. To rewrite the lie that trauma is destiny.

Because it's not.

I now know: the dirt road wasn't just a setting—it was the test. It taught me grit. It taught me empathy. It taught me the kind of father I wanted to become, and the kind of legacy I didn't want to leave.

The dirt road taught me survival. But the highway ahead—that's where purpose lives. That's where healing takes the wheel.

And that's what *Pathways* is about.

Pathways, my next book, picks up where The Dirt Road leaves off. It dives into what I learned during that fifteen-year gap. It also explores what comes after the trauma—how we rebuild, how we move forward, how we lead without repeating the cycles we inherited. It's not about perfection. It's about perseverance. It's about stepping into adulthood with all its uncertainty and still choosing hope, still choosing growth, still choosing to show up—especially on the hard days.

Because healing isn't a destination. It's a path. Sometimes winding. Sometimes uphill. But always worth taking.

If The Dirt Road was my way of making peace with where I came from, then *Pathways* is my way of honoring those who guided me along the way—and inviting others to walk alongside me

If you're reading this and your past still haunts you, know this: you're not alone. You don't have to carry the full weight forever. You're allowed to set it down. You're allowed to heal. You're allowed to keep going.

And maybe, just maybe, the cracks in the pavement are where the light gets in. Every detour, every wrong turn, every breakdown—it all becomes part of the map. You're not lost. You're learning how to find your way.

Life is a highway. And no matter where you've come from, the road ahead is still yours to drive.

THE
DIRT ROAD

Ralph "Cooter" Davis

The Beginning

Rainy Day Adventures

Car Battery Power Wheel

1989 Snowman

Chip

Adam

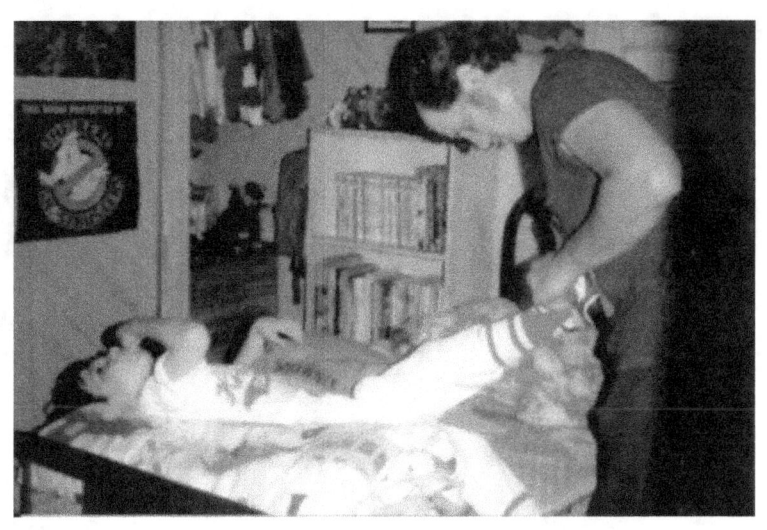

Baseball

Pinewood

The Trailer

The Playhouse

The Farmhouse & Porch

The Beartrap Barn

AUTHOR BIO

 **Robert Hendry** is a Southern-born author, corporate athlete, and executive leader with over 30 years of experience in business and community engagement. He has led a $100+ million business and directed marketing operations across the Southeast for a Fortune 500 company, in addition to spearheading community relations efforts in partnership with nonprofits, NGOs, and government agencies to drive meaningful impact.

With unflinching honesty and a heart for resilience, Robert writes to encourage those navigating pain, purpose, and the pursuit of lasting peace.
His debut memoir, *The Dirt Road*, is a powerful reminder that our beginnings may shape us, but they do not define us—and that healing is always within reach.

To connect or learn more, visit roberthendrybooks.com.

www.ingramcontent.com/pod-product-compliance
Lightning Source LLC
Chambersburg PA
CBHW060128130626
46556CB00006B/2267